THEY CALLED ME
NECKTIE N-WORD

Tibor Sturm

About the book:

Already as a small child I got used to hiding my feelings. My smile became a disguise with which I tried to protect myself. But with every humiliation, every offense, I became angrier. This is how an angry Black child became a teenager and eventually an angry Black man. This book provides an insight into my life. It depicts the harsh reality of Black people in Germany.

About the author:

Tibor Sturm is an anti-racism coach, an emigrant, an immigrant, a refugee from his home country, a seeker of a new home and, above all, a Black German without Black roots. He was a rapper with Brothers Keepers e. V., an actor and has become a loving family man after a seemingly neverending odyssey. He needed to write this book to gain a bit of internal peace and freedom.

THEY CALLED ME
NECKTIE N-WORD

A Black child in white Germany

Tibor Sturm

1st Edition, 2020

Table of Contents

Preface

Welcome to my world. It was often cruel – and still is. As ugly as the face of racism that many are enduring each and every day. This book is part of my personal history. It deals with my childhood and adolescence in Franconia. A white Middle Franconia. A white town called Lauf an der Pegnitz, my birthplace.

I tell it in episodes. The story is not presented in chronological order. I leafed through old diaries to write down my thoughts. Hypnosis sessions brought to light very deep memories. With this book I am not accusing anyone and I am not defending myself. I depict the events as they happened for me. It is my view of things. I still can't talk about much of what happened back then. I have managed, however, to write about it. It has been a healing process. For Black people, the world is often harsh. They experience discrimination, physical and psychological violence, racism in all circumstances over and over again. Experiencing and understanding this is not easy for *white* people living in a *white* majority society. I am aware of that. If you, as a reader, nevertheless take on this challenge, you have my solidarity. Thank you for embarking on this journey. Maybe it will have an effect on you and the day will come when what you have read will help you. I especially thank my wonderful wife and wild children. Thank you for allowing me to write a book again and for giving me the time for this.

*Notes:

Some names of people involved and locations have been changed for privacy reasons and to protect the individuals. M. stands for the woman who gave birth to me.

I have deliberately chosen the spelling n*****. Nobody should refer to Black people with the racist n-word. That's why I neither use it nor write it out.

I deliberately capitalize Black. The term is a self-denotation and refers to people's experiences of racism.

White is written in italics. It is a political description and does not refer to the color of the skin.

1. At the beginning there was the name

1975. I was born on a late Monday evening in early September. M. probably told me about the birth countless times. But I seem to have buried the memories of those conversations deep inside me. What I haven't forgotten is the weird story about how I got my given name, Tibor. When it was certain that a baby was on the way, M. put a lot of thought into the first name. On the one hand it should be "exotic" on the other hand the Franconian people should be able to pronounce it. At the end of the 1960s there was a spin-off of the Tarzan comic series. This series was called "Tibor, Hero of the Jungle". M. thought it was easy enough to pronounce and sufficiently exotic. Still, it's completely unclear to me why it couldn't have been an American first name. Steven, for example, was already known in Germany in the 70s. I'm not unhappy about Tibor — it's just that throughout my life a lot of people have addressed me in Hungarian or asked me whether I come from Hungary. Tibor is a very common name there. If I had been a girl, I would have been called Daniela or Nina by the way.

Of course, I have no memories of my time as a baby or toddler. But I can reconstruct some of it from stories. The most influential one: M. could not love me the way a mother loves her child. I suspect it was a social attachment disorder. It was not until many years later that I learned where this came from, and the revelation was a first deep cut in my life. In any case, my grandmother and her sister told me that M. never really got used to me. The city pastor interfered very early after my birth and "counseled" her during her pregnancy. Exactly what those counseling sessions were, like much else, remains a mystery to this day. I only know that much: as a newborn I was said to have cried a lot and for a long time. Of course, when baby crying is frequent and persistent, it becomes a major cause of stress. Add to that the fact that the baby wasn't wanted and you may even regret giving birth to the little creature in the first place, and every sound from that tiny mouth weighs even more heavily. To make matters worse, M., the woman who carried me inside and gave birth to me, was a single mother with a "n***** baby" in the fall of 1975. That, my grandma told me, was how some citizens of Lauf referred to me when they saw me in the baby carriage.

At 19, M. was not only a young woman who became an unwanted mother – her baby also had dark skin. All the photos that exist of me as a newly hatched human being show me sleeping or smiling. An angel of a baby, were there not the many stories about me as a cry baby. But it fits the picture, because in my family they did everything to keep up the appearance of an ideal world. Today I am sure that none of it was true.

My grandmother was the family patroness, with a very big heart. She looked after everything and everyone in our house, she herself had six children by five men. So she was almost certainly a great exception in a small Franconian town in the 1940s to 1960s. Some of the men involved were American GIs. Accordingly, two of my uncles and an aunt were fathered by three *white* U.S. soldiers. When I was born, none of these "occupier" fathers was around anymore. We lived with my great-grandmother, one of my two aunts and the youngest uncle (he is only eleven years older than me) in a ground-floor three-room apartment in the south of the city of Lauf. M. soon went back to work and so other people looked after me from time to time. They all told different stories about my nature. For some I was an ordinary baby who only cried when my diaper was full or when I was hungry. For others, I was a baby who wailed and cried all the time and rarely found peace. Today I will not fathom which of the depictions was true and it does not play a significant role in my life anymore. It is quite different with my conception. Two stories about it stick persistently in my head and they have been a permanent ordeal for me for decades. However, first of all this is about the first year of my life and thus the beginning of my unusual biography.

Before I was conceived, M. was often seen in the popular clubs of Nuremberg. That ended abruptly when I developed in her belly. Probably, as a pregnant woman and young mother, she always had the feeling that she was missing out on something. As different as the stories about the first year of my life were, there was consensus on one matter: M. was an unmarried young woman with a dark-skinned child in a small Franconian town in

1975. The people of the city of Lauf bad-mouthed M.'s relations with men, which must have been very upsetting for them. After all, the old, traditional way of thinking prevailed at the time: first the house, then marriage, and last but not least, offspring.

M. was unable to handle me. The love she displayed to me always seemed strained, almost forced. Crazy enough, I can even understand that, if the story of my life is true. It is also possible that the social chill I experienced as a baby and child had its origin in Johanna Haarer's pedagogy. In the book "The German Mother and Her First Child," she describes how a child is first broken by deprivation of love and affection, and then made to grow into a "strong" person. If a baby or toddler cries, one should let it do so and only reengage with it when it has calmed down. Hugs or gestures of affection are taboo. No wonder Haarer was something like Hitler's chief educationalist. National Socialist mothers raised mindless infantry with such educational methods. The book was a bestseller long after National Socialism – and ended up with my grandmother, among others. I don't know if M. read the book but she adopted the behaviors of a Harrer's German mother. The family helped M. in everyday life – especially in maintaining a seemingly intact facade. We belonged to the Lutheran parish and there they cared about us – especially about me, this special, foreign-looking child. Without the parish and Pastor Albert (†), I probably wouldn't have seen the light of day. He finally intervened when there were more and more difficulties, for which I was probably held responsible as a baby. In 1976 I was temporarily taken away from M. and placed in a foster family. I was only about ten months old. The Schmidts' apartment, as the family was called, was only a four-minute walk from our actual home. Still, it was hard for M. to keep her appointments. M. had to come in the evenings or weekends, as is the rule with removed children, and "get used to me." Sometimes she managed, sometimes she didn't. But what could one expect from a young woman who was virtually persuaded to become a mother?

So I lived with foster family Schmidt well before my first birthday. Hans Schmidt was a journalist and covered the globe. He traveled the countries of the world in a big pink camper van and wrote reports about the Middle East, North Africa and so on. The Schmidts play a central role with regard to my own racializing. When I visited them again in the early 80s, I became aware of the role my being Black played in my life and the power differences that existed with *white* people. One thing is certain: The back and forth of my childhood made me restless and internally unstable. Throughout my life, I kept asking myself, "What world was I born into and why am I like this?" The starting point of this confrontation was certainly my time with the Schmidts.

It remains a mystery to this day why I first came to the Schmidts, only to leave them again in 1977. Anyway, I came back to M. and her husband, my father Eduard. She had married him during my absence in 1976.

Until then, great-grandma's three-room apartment with the wood-burning stove in the kitchen had been the center of family life. This was where people met, gossiped and smoked heavily. If M. had also smoked and drunk during pregnancy, I was lucky: I suffered no mental or physical damage. Well, the time in great-grandma's apartment, with my aunt and the youngest uncle was long gone from then on. We moved with Eduard into our own apartment in the west of the city of Lauf, in Nuremberg Street to be exact. Legally, Eduard is my stepfather. But what he has done for me in my life and what he has achieved in me is at least as much as a caring biological father does for his offspring. Eduard was a good ten years older than M.. He had a strong physique, sideburns, a full mustache, thick hair, and calm observant eyes peered out from behind his glasses. He worked shifts in a caring profession and, for as long as I can remember, was even-tempered and understanding. If you look dispassionately at my escapades in my teenage years, he was sometimes too forgiving. Even as a toddler, at about two years old, I began to disobey rules and guidelines. I was told that I was incredibly "stroppy" and often "fussed" when I didn't get my way. I was said to have been a stubborn child. Today I think this is a normal reaction to behavior from those around me. Children test their limits. When Eduard came to us, it became quieter at home. In pictures from that time, I clearly recognize the fatherly closeness of him to me. I laughed in almost every photo with my father – in every photo with M. I have a serious expression. It says a lot to always show such a dead serious face as a two-year-old in the presence of a certain person.

Except for two traumatic incidents at the ages of four and six, I have no memory at all of my time as a small child. When friends tell me how they were comforted by their parents when they would fall down or hurt themselves, I'm fishing in the mud. My memory remains dark. Sometimes I think M. also tried to comfort me. She tried to acknowledge and love me. At times it worked. But a feeling of inner emptiness remains in me as for my mother.

2. The forgotten child

When I was three years old, I joined the Protestant kindergarten "Brücke Regenbogen" (Rainbow Bridge) in Luitpold Street, located in the city of Lauf. The kindergarten teacher Susanne B. (†) took me to her heart from the very beginning. The other kindergarten teacher was suspicious of me. For Sister Mathilde, the nun, I was too quiet and watchful a child. And for Susanne, the second kindergarten teacher, I was just an anxious little chap. Maybe this was due to the fact that as an only child I had not been in touch with any other children. Until then, all my playmates had been much older. There was my uncle, who was eleven years older, or the children in the yellow apartment building in Nuremberg Street, where we lived. Here I had my very own room with colorful wallpaper and a children's bed all to myself. In my great-grandmother's three-room flat, we had shared the rooms with several other people. That never bothered me. On the contrary. My relatives told me that I needed some noise and the conversations of the people around me to fall asleep quickly. I then found my first friends at the day care center. We spent many afternoons and weekends together over the years. There were Alfred, Martin, Florian and

Steffen. Alfred was the naughtiest boy of our clique, even in kindergarten. He was a real rascal. His round face with the eyes close together, always on the lookout for mischief – that attracted me magically. Like many other toddlers in the group, Alfred regularly addressed me with the n-word. I got used to it. I still remember sitting in the morning meeting with the group when I was four years old. As kindergarten students, we were supposed to describe each other, stating the qualities we liked or disliked about the person. When it came to me, one child shouted loudly, "Tibor is a n*****!" The others laughed and I felt a deep feeling of insecurity. Susanne took me in her arms and comforted me. I remember every detail of that affectionate gesture. Never before had anyone protected me against a "threatening" situation. The laughter and the fingers pointing at me hit me deep in the core. Like a wounded deer, I looked around, frightened and uncertain, and at the same time an angry feeling welled up inside me. Susanne probably sensed that it was boiling inside me and took me in her arms firmly. I felt nothing but helplessness, but I also memorized the feeling of security and warmth in a cold environment.

The fact that I remember kindergarten as a cold place may also have to do with the lack of a connection to M.. Several times she forgot me in the center. So there I was, completely dressed, sitting on the bench in the foyer. When it got dark and still no one came to pick me up, Susanne took me upstairs. She lived in the apartment directly above the kindergarten. She had a fluffy carpet, a small living room table, a double-seater couch and a matching armchair. I then waited in this chair. In fact, I was always picked up at some point, but much later than the latest pick-up time at 5 pm. There were all kinds of excuses for this in my family: Either uncle or aunt had forgotten me or sudden overtime of M. was to blame that she was not on time. Apparently, no one bothered to pick up the phone and make sure that I was really waiting upstairs in the apartment.

A child's love for those in his or her immediate vicinity is always sincere and honest. Children do not judge the failures and shortcomings of adults. Only over the years do you understand when you have experienced violence. Throughout my childhood, physical violence never went beyond the famous "slap on the butt." It only became apparent much later what significance being forgotten at daycare and M's social coldness actually implied for me and my life. Hypnosis sessions were part of my education to become a practitioner for psychotherapy. In these sessions I was able to begin to process the consequences of my early childhood experiences. A feeling that hovered over my life like a sword of Damocles always accompanied me: I'm on my own, I can't rely on anyone. And if I do, I will be forgotten or betrayed. It's all the weirder for me that, despite everything, there were people who helped me. For example, during my first racist experiences. I was about four years old when my godfather took me from Haimendorf, a small village with about 300 inhabitants, up to a mountain called Moritzberg. Haimendorf lies at the foot of this mountain. My grandmother and her friend Adolf lived in the second to last house in the village. My uncle parked the car on the dirt road in front of the estate and so we hiked up the hill one autumn afternoon. About halfway up, three elderly hikers, two men and a woman, met us. After a brief greeting and the following scrutiny of my person, one of the hikers promptly asked, "Can he speak German yet?" My godfather retorted that I could even speak Franconian, the local dialect, since I was born here. There was that feeling from kindergarten again: I didn't understand the situation, but it was quite clear that something was wrong and had gone very wrong. I was a sweet four-year-old boy who just wanted to be in nature and didn't yet understand anything about racism. But prejudiced thinking like that of the hikers has been a huge burden throughout my life. It is shocking for me myself how big a part this has played in my biography. Even though I could not place racist behavior at that time, I can remember another incident very well. I was driving a small pedal go-cart up and down in front of the garages of our apartment block. A man came out of the neighboring gas station and kicked at me with his leg. He meant something like: "Go back home, darkie!". I remember the word "darkie" (in German: bimbo) very clearly, because I had never knowingly heard it before. I knew it meant something bad and in this threatening situation I was full of fear. The guy was a medium height skinny filthy man and no doubt drunk in broad daylight. His narrowed and squinted little eyes flashed with anger. He was pure menace to me. Obviously, since I was a little boy playing alone in a driveway. Suddenly the man stumbled over a low spur. His staggering looked to me like the awkward dancing of a huge guy. I did not understand that he let loose hate tirades on me whilst he was doing this. With shaky steps he staggered towards me. He continued to rant, lashed out with his foot to hit me, lost his balance and fell sprawling on the asphalt. I froze in shock and could do nothing. He stopped short, got up disoriented, and swayed back to the neighboring gas station. It took me an eternity to regain my senses. I started screaming and crying like mad. But no one came to comfort me. So I soothed myself again and continued to drive up and down the driveway as if in a trance. Where did so much anger and hatred for a little boy come from? So much disgust at the color of his skin?

My parents worked full time. Eduard even worked shifts, so after daycare I still often stayed with my great-grandmother in the three-room apartment. My great-grandmother's place was in the south of the city of Lauf an der Pegnitz, as was my kindergarten, seen from our apartment in the west of the city.

I had severe problems with my teeth and so my front four front teeth were removed. This gave me a speech defect. I could not pronounce the letter "R". When I was about five years old, I had to see a speech therapist. After about a year and a half and countless funny word games, I was finally able to speak the rolling "R". Years later, at my confirmation, Pastor Albert told me about the bizarre beginning of my speech therapy sessions. Apparently, I had explained to the speech therapist, "I'm a n*****, so others don't understand me so well when I talk to them." The speech therapist was obviously so shocked by this that she told the clergyman about it. For me, however, the n-word was perfectly normal. After all, in kindergarten and at random encounters with elderly grandpas, people regularly called me that. It bothered me at first, only to dull over time. Racist names, which I was called because of my skin color, were not noticed by M. at all. At least she was certainly unable to cope with that.

M. kept silent about the Black part of my parents, that is,

about my biological father, all her life. I often asked Eduard, my grandmother, M. and my great-grandmother why my skin color was "different". It was not "normal", because around me there were only *white* people. Each time I got the very Christian answer, "You are so dark because God made you that way." So I walked around as God's miracle in this small *white* town and suffered it getting worse and worse for me. After all, I now had to stand my ground against church opponents and atheists. No one else had accepted my family's answer. The older children were the cruelest. They insulted me as "freak", "bastard" or "dirty ni****". One of the boys, let's call him Marian, was particularly perfidious. He befriended me just for show. I was also the exotic one on the playground and everywhere else. I was quite naive and very happy about my older friend. He was my protector against the other big boys and still only had bad things in mind. He explained to me, "Your skin color is only borrowed from God. Whenever you wash, a little of it comes off." The proof, he said, were my lighter palms and soles. I was five years old at that time and the explanation seemed quite logical to me. As time went on, I got a real phobia of washing and the gang had their fun. The climax of this rotten game happened during the summer vacation we spent in Switzerland in 1981. My grandmother, one of my aunts together with her family and my parents were there. The weather was uncomfortable like in England. Since the hotel was on a mountain, the fog often didn't come down from the heights and it drizzled frequently. Marian's story about my washed-off skin color didn't stop getting to me here, either. Since my parents and I had our rooms in the left wing, and the rest of the family on the right side of the hotel complex, here's what happened: When I was supposed to go to the bathroom in the morning, I ran as if stung by a tarantula to the other side of the hotel to my grandmother's room and yelled, "Help grandma, they're trying to wash me again!" Everyone laughed about this and the anecdote stuck with me for many years. My especially Christian aunt Tina thought it was super funny to tell it over and over again at family gatherings. No one understood that this was a damn cry for help from a five-year-old, lost, Black boy with no identity.

At that age, M also dragged me to the pediatrician. I was growing too fast and this needed to be professionally examined. They x-rayed my bones and the doctor concluded that I would grow to be at least six feet tall. M. said that I would probably have problems with my clothes and shoes and that nothing could be done about my growth.   The doctor advised hormone treatment and so I was given injections to suppress my growth. Just imagine: a Black German, 6.8 feet tall! What harm could he have done? So I grew to "only" 6.3 feet. Until 1982, I still stayed regularly at my great-grandmother's house. At that time I probably began to put on a second face. I learned from the family to to grin and bear it. The n-word bothered me more and more. It seemed to be acceptable to call me that and when I, as a little boy, said that I didn't like it, I was immediately told: "I didn't mean anything by that." As time went by, they could screw me with their "no offense". By now, the always friendly-looking Black boy had become a seven-year-old. And I became an angry, impulsive, adolescent guy. Nobody understood me – that made me more and more silent. This ambivalent behavior was to intensify in the following years.

In the spring of 1982, we moved into a terraced house in the city of Lauf links der Pegnitz. It was a small house with an old, musty cellar, a tiny toilet and a separate shower, and a living room with an adjoining kitchen on the ground floor. On the first floor were my parents' master bedroom and my bedroom. The attic was not fully equipped and served as a storage room for cardboard boxes. There was enough space for M., Eduard and me. We even had a little black and white dog, Foxi, who was a small mutt mix the size of a Chihuahua. I liked to go for walks with her, because that way I got to know new kids and always had the hope that they wouldn't freak out at some point and call me the n-word. This also worked with the girls, they were always open and welcoming towards me. The nicest of them all was Tanja. She had a friendly smile for everyone, talked a lot and was not as blunt as the boys. Tanja rang our doorbell many a time and asked if I could take Foxi out. These few hours were very nice for me. Unpleasant, however, were the many afternoon hours on the playground. It was a typical children's playground with a ping-pong table, a sandbox with a slide and climbing frame, and a little wooden house. The teenagers there were nine to ten years older than me. They loitered around, smoked and picked on people. I was a designated victim because I was weaker and dark-skinned. The narrow entrance to the playground was lined with bushes about six feet high. As soon as I biked through there, they chased me. Naturally, I ran or pedaled away like a maniac. I generally managed to get away from them on my bike. On foot, however, I was hopelessly outnumbered by them, so I got kicked or slapped, "because that's how you have to treat slaves when they don't toe the line."

I knew nothing about being a slave at that time. I also thought the sick behavior of the brutal teenagers was normal. Yes, in their eyes I was a serf who existed only to serve them, put out the fags, open the beer cans, or dance like a monkey. Every time I had to do one of these humiliating tasks, I wished I had superpowers. Like for many other kids, Superman was totally awesome for me. The movie came to our home on VHS videotape in the early 80s, and I just wished I could be like the guy in the cape. A Regular Joe with laser eyes and other skills who draws on those powers in times of need to help innocent people. I would have done all that. I would have flown the teenagers who were tormenting me into space tied up tightly in a potato sack and then returned to Earth alone. I would have abandoned them on some lonely planet. The problem: all the superheroes I knew had light skin. So how could I have been one? In moments of greatest need and oppression, I still took refuge in such daydreams. I still can't talk to anyone about the humiliations of that time. I lack the words to describe my feelings in these situations. Most of the feelings can hardly be grasped. There is only one thing I remember clearly: anger! It was always there, when the others humiliated me and took away my dignity. But I could not let out this inner fury. That would have made everything even worse for me. I had no chance against the four to six young people all by myself. That's why I allowed everything to happen to me. When they had had enough, they left the playground laughing and cheering. They warned me that if I told anyone, I would have a really bad time. And their threats had their effect. I kept silent. Anger became my constant companion.

At seven and a half, I was as tall as a nine-year-old child and very chubby. Nowhere could I find anyone as strong as me on whom I could take out my anger. So I took things apart or demolished them. In the beginning, this was liberating, but later it wasn't enough for me. It was obvious that I was starting to change. At home, however, I couldn't talk about my experiences and fears. My skin color was a taboo. I once asked M. why it was possible that God had made me different but allowed all the mean things to be done to me. She replied that I was just imagining it – no one was mean to me. The conversation ended.

During the summer vacations I had the playground to myself, because the young racists were all away. One day I sat on the ping-pong table and looked at the adjacent high-rise building. I spotted a man there, about 70 years old, who waved at me. At least that's what I thought. The man lived on the second floor and the balconies faced the playground. I walked out onto the lawn of the property where the apartment building stood and finally heard the words he said while waving: "Sieg Heil – Hail Fuhrer – You belong in Auschwitz!" I did not understand what else he was saying and since it made no sense to me, I went back to the playground. I already knew the "Sieg Heil" from the teenagers. However, I had no idea what it meant and thought it was a part taken from a soccer song. Here, of all places, in an environment that had been largely spared denazification, M. gave birth to a dark-skinned child. And then she also raised it as if National Socialists had never existed. At almost eight years old, I didn't have the slightest idea about being Black or Nazis. I grew up with Roger Whittaker, Nana Mouskouri and many other pop stars. I was often ashamed of my skin color because it seemed like a disfigurement in my *white* environment and I perceived it as such. In many situations, I didn't belong. This also made me imprudent and angry. So I was a young, impulsive, dark-skinned and overweight guy – with no identity or orientation. Anyone could tell me what they thought was right – and I believed it at first. I was the dumb looking Black guy on the lookout in Asterix or the good-for-nothing, never-do-well of a shoeshine boy.

"Come on, n*****, clean my shoes"" is the refrain of a song by Hans Söllner that people liked to attribute to me. *White* guys thought it was hilarious to ask me to shine their shoes in front of their buddies. And it wasn't just kids and teenagers who celebrated this musical filth. Whether it was at campfires or beer-fueled celebrations, I was frequently teased with this song throughout my childhood and adolescence. The n-word was normal in my world as a way of identifying myself as "special" and "different". No matter how it was meant by Söllner, the vile song branded me in my most innocent time and made me a hunted person.

The summer vacations came to an end and I was enrolled to school one year later than usual. Myself and no one else could even begin to fathom what school had in store for me.

3. Tibor the liar

I started school four days after my eighth birthday. On September 12, 1983, I walked into the first grade of the Bertlein School. The school building was only a five-minute walk from our house. Eduard and M. accompanied me on the first day of school. The large entry gate with long stairways and a ramp merged seamlessly into the covered school entrance. Because of the concrete ceiling, it was always dark in this area, which was about ten yards long. On the right was the school for special education, which later played a minor role in my school career. On the first day of school, however, my eyes were wide and full of curiosity. In the assembly hall there were rows of chairs in front of a podium and we took our seats. The principal greeted us solemnly and after his speech we were led to the class in the basement.

A tall lady stood by the door and introduced herself as our class teacher, Ms. Bauck. I was assigned a seat in the second row by the window. I sat there with my huge school bag, my dark blue sweater on top of my light blue shirt, my dark blue corduroy pants with 70s cuffs, and brown leather shoes. Ms. Bauck asked what we wanted to become when we grew up. Steffi wanted to be a shop assistant and Daniela a veterinarian. When it was my turn, I said that I wanted to be as tall as our teacher. Since the parents were still standing in the classroom, everyone laughed. I laughed along out of embarrassment and once again understood nothing. However, I liked the role of the comedian and clown more and more. So I was the center of attention of my *white* classmates and was well liked.

Unlike the other children from my old kindergarten group, I ended up in class 1a. Fortunately, I rarely saw the kids from class 1b anymore in the playground and during vacations. The *white* group dynamic of the children was overwhelming. For example, when we were told to bring skin-colored crayons the next day and I then dragged in this pale pink paint, a few kids laughed and told me to use my color: "dirty brown." Helplessly, I tried again to laugh away my pain.

Class hours were for looking out the window and counting butterflies. When there were no butterflies, I counted blades of grass. The large window panes were in front of the leafy, diagonally rising light shaft through whose barred openings the light shone. I became a daydreamer. I dreamed myself into a world without the nasty looks and words of the grandmas on the way home during the many boring lessons. Precisely at the end of the school day, the two elderly ladies were hanging around their basement windows. As soon as they saw me, they cussed that I should quickly disappear. After all, n****** stole like magpies and I would only ruin their beautiful flowers. The plants were hanging down their windows in plastic flower boxes and would have been out of my reach, but that wasn't the women's concern. For them I was the embodiment of the enemy occupier. The oppressor and destroyer of their high German culture. The enemy. The swastika flags in one grandmother's living room testified to what sort of person she was. From the street, everyone could see the flag in the apartment quite clearly but no one cared. The other grandma had purple hair with a fierce perm. Her husband, I knew, had been shot by a US soldier during the war. So I was the catalyst for her trauma. Every day I had to pass by the grandmothers' houses when I went to see my great-grandmother. She took care of her first-grade great-grandson when M. and Eduard were working. My great-grandma Grete was born in 1900, so she had lived through two world wars. Despite her 83 years, she was in top shape – on foot and in her mind. Maybe she told me something about World War II and the Nazis, but I can' t remember any of that.

In the course of the first school year I became more and more of an outsider. Although I had no problems to complete all tasks satisfactorily, my annual report said that I was distracted easily. In addition, I prevented others from participating in class. I had a " vivid personality".

The first summer vacations as a student we spent for two or three weeks in Hungary at Lake Balaton. Because of my Hungarian first name, many who overheard it immediately addressed me in Hungarian. I smiled sheepishly and wished myself away from that place. Some people reacted aggressively when I just shrugged my shoulders without understanding. When we were back in the city of Lauf, I often hung around in the afternoons with my buddies from kindergarten days. We rode our bikes through the neighborhood and Artur, the boy who was already conspicuous in kindergarten, annoyed people and made their blood boil. Sometimes I joined in his pranks. Once we offered to carry an elderly lady's shopping bag home. Then we pretended to run away. Her horrified look when she saw her week's groceries disappear gave us a bellyache from laughter. We basically apologized with an excuse and then actually carried the groceries all the way home. Other than that, I managed to escape my tormentors very successfully during the vacations. If my friends didn't have time in the afternoon, I would lie around in our little garden or play with Steffi, the neighbor girl.

At the end of the vacations, just before I entered the second grade, M. took me to the hairdresser. The salon was located opposite the bank in Altdorfer Street. The hairdresser greeted me with, " Now, are we going to trim that jungle head again?" I nodded in a friendly pained manner. I was already used to this greeting. My hair was an attraction anyway. Elderly ladies, who admired my brown skin sympathetically, ran their hands through my afro curls without being asked and tousled them wildly. I was extremely uncomfortable, but no adult would speak up for me, and I myself lacked the right words. And again anger was boiling in helpless Tibor. I laughed sheepishly and tried to get out of the way quickly. This reaction made sure that I became known as a dear and nice guy. The hairdresser used to hand me my jungle head hair in a bag and I used to make pictures with it. I drew stick figures and glued my hair on their heads. The figures were generally *white*. That's when I started hating the color of my skin. Because of it and my little black curls, I was insulted, groped, humiliated and outlawed. In addition, my unpredictable "friends" were a real burden. When I was alone with them, they behaved unremarkably. But as soon as others from the clique were around and the mood heated up, everything was like it used to be in daycare. I was again the n***** and darkie. Ms. Bauck had health problems, so we got a new class teacher in the second grade, Mr. Sieben. Mr. Sieben was a thin, short man with a crown of black hair. In the introductory round, he asked for our names and ages. When it was my turn, a new classmate interrupted. "Tibor is a n*****," he yelled, laughing out loud. The boy's name was Peter and he came from the neighboring school for special education. He was from a socially disadvantaged area in the west of the city. The family was known for their foul-mouthed nature. So Peter was now sitting with me in class 2a and had already shown me on the first day of school the way he worked. But Mr. Sieben challenged him. He sternly explained that the n-word was not to be used because it was an insult to people with dark skin. It hit me like a bolt of lightning. What had my teacher just said? That was a bad word? So had I always been justified in having this uncomfortable feeling when people called me that? What was I supposed to do with this new bit of knowledge that was spectacular to me? I was completely overcome. Mr. Sieben saw my confusion and said that he wanted to talk to me after school. I could hardly wait and was shaking with excitement when the time finally came. Mr. Sieben and I were alone in the classroom. I sat at my desk and he pulled up a chair. He looked at me seriously as he asked me where I was from. I explained to him, of course, that I was a boy from the city of Lauf and was also born here. When he inquired about my father and mother, I told him everything I knew. For Mr. Siebert, the matter was then apparently clear. My teacher explained that there were adults who didn't like me because of the color of my skin. And children would adopt the thinking of their parents. He wanted to know if it had been made clear to me where my skin color came from. Of course, I told him the story my family had drilled into me, "God made me this way." Mr. Seven was silent for what felt like an eternity. He probably realized that his little student was wandering this earth cluelessly when it came to Black things. He most likely spared himself any further explanation about Black people so as not to fully disturb the nine-year-old. When we said goodbye, he took another promise from me. Every time someone called me the n-word, I was to come to him and tell him. It was not to last long.

The next day, at first recess, I was standing in line at the kiosk to get my milk. Suddenly, someone grabbed me by the collar from behind and pulled me out of line. I turned around and looked into a hateful face. "You're going to get a spanking, darkie, so you'll know who is the master race!" I was extremely frightened. There were about 30 students in line and everyone was just watching, no one was helping. I was rooted to the spot in front of this guy who was easily a head and a half taller. He was talking to me with his fist raised. Everything seemed like a blur to me. Through the veil I recognized: The attacker was Gustav. Peter's 17-year-old brother. He lashed out, but before his fist hit me, a teacher rushed over and stood between us. Actually, Gustav had no business being here. He had already been expelled from school three years ago. After that, no one else wanted to take him in. Gustav was a skinhead. A Nazi who was known as a mean thug everywhere. His grandfather had been an SS Sturmbannführer and had raised the whole family according to the Fuhrer's view of the world with a lot of violence. In a way, Mr. Sieben was the reason Gustav wanted to rough me up. The day before, he had called the Nazi family and told them that Peter had called me a n*****. The parents objected, claiming that their gentle son would never say such a thing. Of course, they knew better. They just panicked that their little bugger would end up in school for special education again. To prevent that, they unleashed their Gustav on me. The teacher who saved me felt compelled to call the police as well. Gustav did not stop raining down hateful tirades on me. In addition, a huge swastika was emblazoned on his shirt. When the officers arrived, they greeted him like an old acquaintance and took him to the patrol car. I was left scared shitless and a mad fury. Again.

At home, M. was already waiting for me. She asked what I had learned and I told her about math, German and arts and crafts. I kept quiet about the incident with the Nazi. But the rage in me was almost unbearable. My stomach hurt, I had to take it out somewhere. I punched boxes in the attic. That helped. The next day at school, I went to class with an uneasy feeling. I was surprised when Peter came up to me and apologized. But it seemed all iffy. Until the end of the school year, my tension did not ease. But the situation remained calm.

My elderly great-grandmother longed for more rest, so I spent my afternoons with my foster family, the Schmidts, again. They were still very close to me. Not only had I been in their care as a baby, they were also active in our church community.

One day Fred Schmidt brought sheep's wool back from a trip to Africa. I was impressed by the texture – it felt like my hair. My question whether I was related to a sheep was laughingly denied by the Schmidts. But my interest was aroused and I wanted to know everything about Africa. Fred told me about tribes of Black indigenous people, about schools where the Black children wore uniforms, and about rain dance rituals. Fred Schmidt showed me photos from his trips to Africa and that was the first time I saw Black people. From that moment on, I told everyone I was from Africa. I invented my own biography: my ancestors came from mud huts and had lived by hunting. Whether my listeners wanted to know or not, my stories became wilder and wilder and I elaborated on them long and wide. I just had to be careful that people didn't know Eduard and M., to avoid being exposed as a liar. I was lucky and found great pleasure in finally having an identity. If people asked me "Where do you actually come from?", I could answer the questioners in detail. That was the end of the "God made me this way" story. No more "I don't know why I have brown skin." No more hopeless stammering, which was always followed by "Where do your father and mother come from" or something similar. From now on, I received an understanding nod and a smile in response.

"The boy from Africa can already speak flawless Franconian," I often heard. I was a nine-year-old dark-skinned boy who made up stories about his skin color and was somehow acknowledged for his cock-and-bull stories. I didn't understand this insanity, but all that mattered to me was that for the first time I felt good talking about my appearance. If Eduard and M.

ever got wind of my fairytales, they never addressed me about it.

My grandmother moved to her new husband Hannes in the village Haimendorf in 1982. Hannes was a farmer who worked his fields during the day and spent his evenings in the village pub. During my entire life, I exchanged no more than 50 sentences with him. There was an insurmountable distance between us from the very beginning. I could deal with it. After all, I knew this coldness from M.. That's why I concentrated on being with my grandmother. I spent some weekends with her and Hannes. I frolicked over the fields and played Robin Hood or Superman. The wide open spaces and freedom were very good for me. Every Monday morning, Mr. Sieben had us tell him about our weekend. Under no circumstances would I have told him about my innocent heroic games. So I made up exciting stories again, which all my classmates listened to with admiration. My story about the slaughter of a pig went down particularly well. I bragged a lot and told about blood that could have filled three bathtubs. I described the overflowing vat in all its gory detail. Yes, there was blood, blood, blood everywhere in the slaughterhouse. Then I explained how to make blood sausage and cut chops out of a pig's body. The class was thrilled. The truth: I threw up as soon as I entered the slaughterhouse and knew the rest only from grandma's descriptions. As time went on, I didn't feel good about making up stories. To the disappointment of all my classmates, I stopped telling anything about my weekends.

Anyway, the year 1984 passed without the perpetual gauntlet because of my skin color. For my lies, I got something I had never known before – an identity. In the spring of 1985, I was at a flea market in town. Suddenly Gustav appeared. When he caught sight of me, he rushed at me like a berserker. He stopped barely 12 inches in front of me, raised his right arm in salute and shouted "Sieg Heil!" at the top of his lungs. His mouth with the yellow-brown teeth twisted into a dirty laugh. Gustav was fresh out of juvenile detention. Apparently he had not yet realized that his brother and I were getting along in the meantime. Before he could really get at me, two strong men had him in their grip. One of them told him in a low tone that he had better get out of there before the police showed up. Gustav disdainfully gave me the middle finger and disappeared into the crowd. I looked around. It was a familiar situation. Apart from the two men, once again no one had helped me. Instead, many empty faces stared at me. I was to meet Gustav again later under completely different circumstances and would emerge as the winner.

At home, my family didn't show any concern. However, I could not believe that they had not noticed anything about the flea market incident. Because suddenly, for no particular reason, I was given wickedly expensive "Master of the Universe" and "Captain Future" figurines, spaceships, animals and so on. And what did I notice for the first time? All my comic heroes were *white*. Just all of them.

In the summer of 1985, there was a big premiere: I went to the outdoor swimming pool of the city of Lauf all by myself. I biked across the small town and was proud as punch when I got there. I had arranged to meet a few classmates and they were already waiting at the entrance. We found a spot on the lawn, near the deep pool, and immediately jumped into the cool water. Only when our lips were blue and we were shivering did we lie down in the sun to warm up. On the way back from the edge of the pool to the lawn, a wide-eyed woman blocked my path. Without hesitation, she ruffled my hair and exclaimed, stunned, "Gee, your hair doesn't even get wet." I was totally perplexed. I didn't know the woman and didn't even know what she wanted from me. The woman called a friend over and she, too, ran her hands through my hair in disbelief, saying that she wouldn't have thought that of my jungle head. Then I realized who I had in front of me: the hairdressers from Altdorfer Street. My mood was gone and I didn't want to stay anymore. There they were again, these unpleasant situations. I took flight, I left the open-air swimming pool and drove back home. The outdoor pool remained a reservoir of racist experiences for me. Every damn time, someone asked me if I could even get sunburnt. The really stupid ones asked if my lighter palms and feet needed sunscreen. Or they warned me to be careful not to get any darker. Then everyone laughed. Yes, the unchangeable fact that I had more melanin and therefore a darker skin color was a huge joke to my acquaintances. The older I got, the more I became desperate about my appearance. That was understandable, because people were constantly grabbing me or commenting on my skin color. Yet by what right? Children on the playground said that I should go back to Taka-Tuka-land to my n*****king and alluded to Pipi Longstocking's father Ephraim. Others wanted me to give them a "N****kuss" (German pejorative term for a small chocolate-covered cake filled with foamy sugar) on the cheek and laughed out loud. I was left speechless and it made me angry.

Since I had made up the story about my African relatives a year ago, one thing had gotten extremely worse. The hair incident in the open-air swimming pool demonstrated it: the people around me were becoming physically assaultive. This brought me to the edge of despair. I distrusted the *white* people around me more and more. Because as soon as I opened up in the slightest, I was no longer safe from touches that made me uncomfortable. They touched me, my hair, my skin. I didn't like myself, and I especially didn't like the color of my skin. I wanted to be *white* like my comic book heroes, my schoolmates, the people on TV and in the city of Lauf. But I couldn't. As I had no one to share my thoughts with, as no one saw my suffering and talked to me about it, I withdrew. Actually, it was not in line with my nature at all, but the summer of 1985 was the summer in which I became a very introverted person.

The necktie-n***** and the ruler

In third grade, we got another new teacher. The new one was the complete opposite of Mr. Sieben. Mr. Fänger was an elderly *white* man with only a few years left until retirement. I had a massive growth spurt during the summer vacation. By now I was about 5.4 feet tall. Mr. Fänger was a good 5.5 feet and when we faced each other we made for a pretty odd sight. My new class teacher was an ardent fan of the old German language and had us cram many words that were not familiar to us in German class. We were only allowed to say "Steckenpferd", the old-fashioned expression for "hobby" or "Klamauk" instead of play time. Mr. Fänger was also old-fashioned in his punishments. He had a 19 inch long ruler that he misused for other purposes. Every time the students violated his rules, talked loudly or disturbed the class in any other way, he would bang the ruler noisily on the table. I often liked to chat with Alfred, so the ruler banged right past the tip of my nose on the school desk a couple of times a day. Unlike me, my seatmate didn't hold back his emotions and was very impulsive. And so, one day, a heated exchange of words between Alfred and our teacher led to disaster. Mr. Fänger unjustly accused my classmate of having been chattering. Alfred defended himself, and with every word back from his student, the teacher became more and more infuriated. It turned wild. The heads of the two ran equally high red. Alfred angrily straightened up, and the teacher took a swing at him to carry out his table-banging action. Suddenly Alfred's arm went up and caught the ruler before it whizzed down. He pulled it out of Mr. Catcher's hand, grabbed it in both of his hands and broke it. The classroom was eerily silent. Alfred had tears in his eyes and ran out, snorting with rage. The girls were shocked. Especially Tanja. Normally she was always in a good mood, but now her smile gave way to a serious and worried expression. Only one boy was laughing like crazy: Christopher, my archenemy. He was a beefy guy who was well received by the girls because of his wiald nature. He liked to wear thick sweaters and tight jeans, which made him look even more chunky and muscular. His voice was already deeper than the rest of us boys and on the playground he smoked his first cigarettes. Christopher always wanted to be the boss. He loved to insult me, and as an outsider, I was the perfect victim for him.

While I suffered in school, it was actually a good year in

terms of family. We undertook a lot with friends and regularly went to Himmelgarten, a beautiful place near the city of Lauf. I was still in elementary school but I already had a little hunch about love. I had my first crush in the first grade. Her name was Christina, she had blond curls and big blue eyes. She looked like the Nuremberg Christkind. Every afternoon, I made up my mind to approach her the following day and ask if we might be friends. When the moment came, I couldn't produce a sound and didn't work up the courage. Christina's family moved in the middle of the school year and off she went. I suffered a lot and needed a long time to fall in love again. Then in Himmelgarten it was finally happening. Dorothea was the daughter of a family who was friends. With her curly red hair and blue-green eyes, she was incredibly cute. Our parents liked to meet at an inn that was located on a small hillside. There was a meadow at the bottom and the whole area was surrounded by tall trees. There the two of us sat and watched the fireflies buzzing around us. We held hands and smiled at each other. And then on one of those mild early summer nights, it happened. We looked into each other's eyes for a moment and she gave me my first kiss. Doro was a sweet and kind girl who never insulted me or made fun of my skin color. We had known her parents from the apartment in Nuremberg Street. They also lived in the high-rise building and her mother Christa possessed a strong personality. But for reasons I didn't understand, my parents stopped seeing Christa after the kiss. That was the end of my crush. Shortly after that, Doro moved.

We traveled a lot that year. Sometimes I accompanied Eduard and M. to friends' houses or to a restaurant, sometimes

I stayed with my grandmother in the village of Haimendorf. I was a latchkey child and when I had school, I was often alone with Foxi at home in the afternoon. After homework I took her for a walk. Together we walked along Hofmann Street to Flur Street. There was an undeveloped area with tall, hollowed-out bushes and a lot of grassy area. Foxi ran around and did her business. The rear part of the compound was almost impenetrable with dense shrubs. Often I heard an eerie rustling sound. There were countless creepy stories about the site. Supposedly homeless people lived there and we kids were told to stay away. But for an adventurous kid like me, the thrill of the forbidden was tremendous. So one afternoon I took Foxi on a tight leash and followed the rustling in the hedges. I inched closer and pushed aside a few branches. One bush had been accurately hollowed out and was surely giving shelter to some homeless person. I looked around cautiously and noticed some weird magazines. I grabbed one and looked at it curiously. There were soldiers on the cover. Many of the letters had the strange writing that Mr. Fänger also showed us in the old books. I carefully turned the page with a twig. There it was again: the swastika like the one in the living room of the grandma who insulted me. By now I knew it was the symbol for something bad and looked around fearfully. There were jagged Rambo knives and baseball bats everywhere. I was horrified. Where the hell had I landed? I quickly made a run for it. On the way home, the same question kept pounding in my head, "Why is this sign following me?" To this day, I don't understand why there are still people who glorify Hitler and his wretched Nazi ideology. What is it about some Germans that is so screwy that makes them chase after a hopeless idiocy of racial mania?

As the school year progressed, Mr. Fänger became more and more hostile. Alfred had not hesitated a second. After his argument with the teacher, he ran straight to the principal and told him that he had broken Fänger's ruler out of fury. This action brought our teacher's disciplinary sanctions to light. From now on, he was no longer allowed to use a ruler to attract more attention in the class. Mr. Fänger had always been a bad-tempered person and I had a hard time getting decent grades. At the parents' evening in the second half of the year, he said very clearly that he could not give me a recommendation for grammar school because I could hardly keep up in class and would absolutely not meet the necessary requirements. Of course, my parents followed this recommendation and I was not registered. I was furious. This was because Mr. Fänger told me to my face what he thought of me. He said that I could possibly make it, but that such a vermin as I was had no place in a grammar school. I should be happy if I didn't end up in a school for special education. When I talked about it one evening at home, nobody believed me. M. blamed it on my vivid imagination, after all, no teacher would say such a thing. That was the end of the discussion. M. accused me of laziness because of my mediocre grades and that I should try harder. I came to terms with this and my distrust of *white* people inevitably grew once more. After all, I had more than enough experiences: those mean elderly people, the nasty teacher, and some of the students who made my life miserable. And if I wanted to bring up a racist incident with my parents, I was made out to be a liar. That drove me up the wall.

My comfort would be family gatherings with Eduard's relatives. The celebrations of M.'s family were more frequent, but I did not like them so much. One family member had it in for me there. Walter, my grandmother's nephew, had a drinking problem. Whenever he was drunk – at every party – he let the Aryan of the family hang out. Then he would say things like "You're not one of us," or "Go back to where you came from". My grandmother caught this a few times and then told him to be quiet. Other than that, no one ever talked about it. The only people who occasionally told me about racism were the Schmidts. But they had also moved away from the city of Lauf in 1985. I only had occasional interactions with my peers – they had made fun of me and insulted me too often. But I was tired of being alone and was looking for a friend. In the city of Lauf an der Pegnitz there are three big church festivals: the "Hämmernkirchweih" (celebration of the church saint), the Laufer Altstadtfest (old town festival) and the "Kunigundenkirchweih" (another celebration of a church saint). The latter featured a proper procession on Sundays and on Mondays that led right through the town to the mountain called Kunigundenberg. Almost the entire town stood on the sidewalks on both days and applauded. There were daycare groups dressed up in costumes, the men's group of the "sooty ones" (in former times, these were the tool smiths who also protected the castle walls in case of imminent danger), flower floats, the newly appointed Kunigunde on horseback, who was elected every year, and also the TSV Lauf marching band. My youngest uncle Martin was also among the latter. We stood near my much hated hairdresser when the men and women dressed in red with their instruments passed by us. The loud music, the satisfied looks of the troupe – I was blown away. I really wanted to be a part of this fascinating group. I also told my parents that. They talked to Martin and he took me to a practice session on a Friday without further ado.

The reception in the marching band was friendly from everyone without exception. For the first time I really felt welcome and accepted. Apart from three later incidents, this feeling was in fact never to disappear. After the practice session, some would visit the neighboring inn to eat, drink and chat. It was all so awesome for me. From then on, there was only one goal for me: to become a tenor horn player in the marching band. During the children's practice sessions on Friday afternoons, I got to know Olaf and Heiner. Olaf had two sisters, one older and one younger. Heiner had an older brother. They were all in the marching band. We became friends very quickly and met outside of practice hours to ride our bikes. During the summer vacations, the two boys first went to the annual camp. After that we biked through the villages of the area. Heiner and Olaf were three years older than me and that in itself was great. But after the vacations I began the 5th grade.

A new game had found its way into the playground: Who's afraid of the bogeyman (in German: "Schwarzer Mann" = Black man)? Of course I was the Black man. Because that was obviously too lame for my classmates, they kept changing the chant. Who is afraid of the slave man? Who is afraid of the Bimbo (= Darkie) Man? And so on. At the same time, the words of the game don't make any sense at all. It is always the same dialogue: "Nobody!" – "And if he comes?" – "Then we run away!". "If you're not afraid, why are you running, you idiots?",

I often shouted back. But this incited them even more. During many breaks, everyone stood around me, trying to get me to freak out. Right in the forefront again was Christopher.

Fall 1985: One afternoon we were invited to a gathering of my father's family right after school. I had to get dressed up and was not allowed to stain myself at all. So I showed up for class wearing dark blue pants, a white shirt with a yellow cardigan, and a matching yellow leather tie. During the first break, I didn't dare go out in the yard at all, but flailed around in front of the classroom on the ground floor. Just before recess was over, Christopher came up to me and said loud and clear, "From now on, you're the Neck Tie-N*****!" I had long since lacked the vigor to respond to such verbal attacks. I literally felt dead inside. Within me, anger and helplessness combined, but I didn't care. I would have liked to ram Christopher into the ground, but I was afraid of the consequences, so I didn't bother. The name quickly circulated and in almost every break somewhere it echoed: "Neck Tie-N*****!". I didn't talk about it with anyone. When I sought help, the response was too bad. So I bottled up the frustration.

I no longer enjoyed anything. Everything was literally driving me up the wall. One day I was walking through the streets of the neighborhood, passed the gas station in Altdorfer Street, turned into Niebelungen Street and after about 50 yards I stopped in shock. On the other side of the street there stood a Black man in traditional African attire, like I once saw in the pictures of the Schmidts. I didn't know what to say or do. With wide, disbelieving eyes, I remained rooted to the spot. The man laughed amiably and showed his gleaming white teeth. I still could not move and so he beckoned me to him. I was full of respect and did not dare to cross the street. He called his name to me before he disappeared into the entrance of the house. His name was Mufasa Mufasa. He had the same first and last name. This encounter fascinated me a great deal and briefly distracted me from all the bad things that had happened in the last few weeks. The more I thought about how to handle the constant insults, the more I came to the conclusion: Mufasa had to know the answer to all my questions. But already with my next breath I felt that deep distrust again. Not even in my thoughts could I confide in anyone. It tore my heart apart. The few good days with my friends and the moments when the school bullies were not there could not compensate for the many insults and bullying. If I had had someone to talk to, many things would have been easier. Of course I had buddies like my classmate Stefan. But they were all *white*. Although we got along well – because of my childhood experiences, I just couldn't really trust light-skinned people. Apparently, I now harbored this distrust toward Black people as well. I longed for an interchange with an elderly Black person to finally get an explanation for all my feelings and experiences. But as soon as the opportunity arose after so many years, I withdrew.

Since I had learned to always put on a friendly face in front of people, no one dreamed of what I was going through inside. The recesses at school and the daily insults from the dumbasses in 8th and 9th grade were wearing me down. Every damn night I cried alone in my room. I was defenseless and had no outlet for my growing anger. Inside, I was numbing out. At night I dreamed wildly and relived the same scenario over and over again. I ran into the dark, away from the light. Behind me I heard all the insulting swear words. I fell into a hole with no bottom. The dream was so real that I often woke up terrified, fled next door to my parents' bedroom and lay down between them. I sought closeness where there was no real intimacy – and I didn't know any other way. This went on throughout the fifth grade. As a ten-year-old, I constantly wondered what was going to happen to me. I decided to focus more on the marching band and less on school. Consequently, my grades got worse, and Mr. Fänger proved me right. However, because I practiced often, I played the fanfare horn better and better. This wind instrument was the preliminary stage to the tenor horn, my instrument of choice. M. did not see my progress. Instead, she reprimanded me. When I came home from practice one evening in the rain and immediately dried my instrument case with a towel, she scolded me for caring more about music than about school. She did not realize how much I was suffering there.

4. Fishing, Franz-Josef and the shock

The 1986 school year started with a highlight. The commuter train from the city of Lauf links der Pegnitz to Nuremberg was officially launched on September 26. The guest of honor was none other than the Bavarian Prime Minister Franz-Josef Strauß. The plot with the bushes, where I found the swastika booklets and knives, had to give way to a "park & ride" parking lot. My parents and I were standing in the parking area, just outside the stairs to the underground passage that led to the tracks. Directly in front of me was a cordon. The crowd was huge and the local news was setting up next to me. Then everything happened very quickly. Suddenly, a couple of men in suits stood in front of me and Franz Josef Strauß stood in the center. He was giving an interview to a journalist, turned to his right, saw me, ran his hand over my head ruffling my hair and said in Bavarian dialect, "You do have beautiful hair." Then he was gone again and I was unbelievably angry and at the same time clueless. "I don't like it," I said, only he had long since gone out of earshot. My parents were proud, and M. asked me if I knew who had been running his hands over my hair. I answered nothing to that, but just smiled sheepishly. Inside me, the anger and distrust became stronger than ever that day. Fortunately my classmates Tanja and Stefan visited me in the afternoon. We talked about Battlestar Galactica, He-Man and Transformers. Tanja and her younger sister Nikki were the best girls and friends you could ask for to distract you. Stefan, too, was an always cheerful boy with an open and liberal home upbringing. In fact, I had always trusted him. I was eleven years old and by now 5.5 feet tall. That made me considerably taller than average. This had advantages and disadvantages. One advantage was that I didn't stand out at all next to my two older friends Olaf and Heiner. The disadvantage was that almost everyone around me thought I was older and talked to me that way. So I had to make an effort and act more grown-up than I would have preferred. At school, I was bored or downright disgusted by teachers and students. I wanted to go to grammar school or at least to a secondary school in order to make it out of the city of Lauf at some point. My hopes were high – and were disappointed.

Mufasa was a friendly Black man. He told me about Africa and how apartheid had almost cost him – a king's son – his life. He found the wife for eternity in Monika, a celebrity from the city of Lauf, and moved in with her. The day he arrived in Lauf was also the day I saw him for the first time. The fame of his wife had a special reason. Monika weighed an estimated 570 pounds. She lived on the second floor of an apartment building in the left hand part of the city of Lauf. When she wasn't feeling well one day, the fire department had to use a crane to remove her from the living room window. The action naturally caused quite a stir. Mufasa took tender care of Monika and they eventually had a daughter. The stories of Mufasa were not all that exciting for me, because he did not give me answers to my most pressing questions. Therefore I did not look for any further contact to him. But suddenly there was another Black boy living in the neighborhood. Melvin had moved to the city of Lauf with his mother from the U.S. base in Kaiserslautern. She had separated from his father, a GI, and wanted to return to her hometown. Melvin was, except for the color of his skin, the exact opposite of me. Too short for his age, skinny and extremely withdrawn. He came to our class and in English class he pronounced the words we were supposed to repeat with a little delay so that everyone could hear his good English. For me, the English language presented a problem. But our English teacher maintained her prejudices and assumed that English was my mother tongue because of the color of my skin. Even though she knew M. and Eduard from the parent-teacher conferences. I crammed English twice as much as my classmates and still got a poor grade. The fact that my efforts were useless made me sad and angry at the same time. I wanted to improve my English, but I didn't want to conform to my English teacher's strange view of the world, in which all dark-skinned people spoke fluent English. The history lessons were also traumatic. In the sixth grade we dealt with pharaohs and pyramids. The latter were built by slaves, and as soon as the subject came up, I was asked about my ancestors. Melvin was out of it, since it was proven that he had an American father. I, however, had made up an African origin. That's why everyone assumed that there had been a slave in my family at some point. By now I was bored with these provocations and no longer reacted to them. This in turn earned me the respect of the new history teacher. He was still a trainee teacher and thought it was great how I dealt with the insults. So mature and detached. Of course, he didn't know that I had already gone through all the emotions in the past years, and I didn't tell him either.

In the marching band I finally got my private tenor horn teacher. Mr. Lehmwand. He was certainly well over 70 years old and had been a teacher for the marching band for ages. Since he was no longer able to walk so well, I had my practice lessons at his home. He lived with his wife in a corner house with a narrow yard and 60s furnishings. Mr. Lehmwand paid meticulous attention to a correct sitting position and a flawless scale. I sat on a soft foam chair and he sat on a wooden chair next to it. At first I enjoyed it very much, but after a while I got bored with the same exercises over and over again. Nevertheless, I pushed through and during the Pentecost vacations I was allowed to practice with the grown-ups on Friday evenings. That was great. The hard work had paid off and I felt very comfortable in the midst of the older companions. Niko, Marion, Ralph and Kerstin were especially friendly and affectionate towards me. Kerstin was Olaf's older sister and Ralph's girlfriend. All were in their mid to late 20's and accepted me as part of the marching band family. I could laugh sincerely there and learned for life. There were Solstice celebrations, camps, youth activities, and in all of it I was a part of the big picture. That felt wonderful. At home, I was the spoiled single child who was increasingly pacified with money. For an eleven-year-old, I got a lot of pocket money from my grandma. I usually used it to buy my way out of the antisocial teenagers from the playground. They were out of my life for some time. But when Melvin moved in right across from the playground and got into a risky situation at some point, I had to step in. From then on, they had it in for me again. Before they humiliated me again, I offered to give them 30 marks a week. They agreed and I paid protection money to stay unharmed. Since grandmother was not always so reliable with the weekly pocket money, I was able to "credit ", but then had to pay crazy interest charges on top of that a week later. What else could I have done? Talking to my parents about it would have only caused more problems. Eduard would have gone to the broken families of the hooligans and would have kicked up his heels there. I would then have gotten the boomerang back in the form of even worse oppression and higher protection payments.

My behavior had changed noticeably in the fall days of 1986. I was erratic, unfocused, loud, and quickly became aggressive. My performance in school, however, got permanently better, contrary to expectations. I longed for winter, because then my oppressors were nowhere to be seen and I could spend a few undisturbed, solitary hours in our small house. The cold had bothered me for ages, but the silence made up for it all. Winter was followed by spring and I was eagerly awaiting the first performance of the marching band. Then I would play the Radetzky march with the shiny gold tenor horn and in the traditional red and black outfit. I wished so much that all the people of the city of Lauf would marvel at me at the Kunigundenkirchweih, the church fair. I loved my uniform. Black shoes, red tights, the black knee breeches, a red heavy outfit with the insignia of the TSV-Lauf and the marching band, plus a big red barrett with a white feather. I didn't care that the tights itched. I just wanted to be a part of this fantastic ensemble. But I had to be patient. It wasn't until the early summer of 1987 that I was allowed to march in the Kunigundenfest. Before that, I had not yet reached my maturity on the tenor horn. I was given a practice period so that I could reliably play the third voice.

Olaf took me to his uncle's carp pond in the city of Schönberg in the spring of 1987. I was terribly excited when he gave me the rod and some quick instruction. I sat down next to my friend in the grass at the edge of the pond and cast the fishing rod, fitted with a kernel of canned corn, into the water. While we waited for the fish to bite, we talked about women. Olaf had a girlfriend who was already of age and drove a car. My interest in women and sex was still limited at that time. That's why our conversations remained rather superficial. In addition, the brake of my fishing rod suddenly started rattling and my pose dropped. I actually had a fish on the line. The fight lasted almost twenty minutes, but in the end I had a seven-kilo carp in the net. I have never had such a feeling of success in my life. I laughed and danced like a little kid. Olaf's uncle took the carp off the hook and threw it back into the pond. Olaf and I were happy. It makes you incredibly happy to have a successful catch. After the lie in wait, the strike comes at the right moment and then, after a short or long drill, the fish lands in the net. I had found a new sport and loved it. On the way back, Olaf's uncle offered us guys to drive a few meters by car across the private property with the large meadow area. My friend didn't want to and slid into the passenger seat. I didn't hesitate, got into the driver's seat, turned the ignition key and off we went. I could only accelerate and brake, I had no idea how to change gears. That's why the poor old Peugeot howled dreadfully in first gear at 22 mph. Uncle Olaf bolted after us in a panic, gesturing wildly. I saw him in the rearview mirror, braked, he caught up with us, yanked open the driver's door and cursed. I don't know what he said, because I was grinning like a Cheshire cat. Fortunately, Olaf's uncle calmed down immediately. He climbed onto the back seat and gave me further instructions from there. Afternoons like that, when I was just happy, were very rare at that time.

Only a week after our fishing trip, I had thick, puffy eyes and was having a hard time breathing. I was plagued by hay fever. M. took me to see Dr. Blendinger. The doctor had just returned from China, where he had learned acupuncture. When he offered me this healing treatment, I immediately accepted. I had extremely bad experiences with the injections of another doctor and could not stand them anymore. As soon as I started the new therapy, I felt better with every week. One day, while I was sitting in the waiting room, a long-haired man in his late 20s approached me. He said he was a physical therapist, among other things, and wondered about my enormously tense muscles. After all, I was only a young teenager. But the man recognized my discomfort from my sequence of movements. That's why he gave me the advice to come to a gym in the neighboring town on Tuesdays. I did, and even skipped my regular tenor horn practice lesson with Mr. Lehmwand to do so. When I arrived by bicycle, two men were standing in front of the hall smoking. They nodded at me as I walked past them into the hall entrance. The building was bright and cheerful inside. There were two wooden benches in front of the equipment locker room and more than half of the training hall was covered with blue mats. I sat down on one of the benches and waited. I waited for things to happen and was amazed at myself. Why did I trust a strange *white* man so much that I dared to enter a gym that was decaying from the outside and completely out of my usual vicinity? What's more, I hadn't told anyone about my trip. I was full of confidence that nothing would go wrong. The fact was, I was simply desperate enough to take such a risk. I was brooding so hard that I didn't even notice some people walking out of the dressing rooms onto the mats and high-fiving each other. The room filled with girls, boys, women and men. Everyone took their places and the short, long-haired man came in. He bowed to the group and they did the same. Then everyone lined up in pairs. One person attacked and the other blocked the blow. I was fascinated by what was going on. The instructor came up to me and greeted me warmly. I was surprised because he obviously knew my name, although I hadn't told him at all when we first met in surgery. But the trainer quickly solved the mystery. My doctor had learned from an elderly patient that the teenage bullies regularly harassed me on the playground. This, in turn, he told the physical therapist friend who was also an acupuncture patient. And since the doctor knew that the long-haired man was a coach for self-defense, he asked him to approach me. Dr. Blendinger had always surprised me in a positive way. He had also found the unusual reason for my allergy. I am actually left-handed by nature, but in elementary school, like so many others, I was drilled to be right-handed. I learned to write with my right hand, but paid a price for it. Due to the constricting change of my natural motor skills, my immune system was attacked. Acupuncture readjusted the physical balance a little. Philipp, that was the instructor's name, explained to me what the old gym was all about. Children and adults alike were given self-defense classes here. The martial arts techniques were a mixture of Jiu-Jitsu and Krav Maga. In Philipp's life story I recognized some parallels to myself. He was Jewish and was repeatedly the victim of anti-Semitic insults and attacks. But then he learned to defend himself and he now taught the martial art to others. I, too, received an invitation to be there again on the following Tuesday, wearing sports clothes. I asked for time to think about it, because actually my musical practice hours were scheduled at that time and the marching band was very important for me. Besides, I wasn't sure if martial arts would really do me any good. After all, my oppressors still outnumbered me, no matter how well I could have defended myself. I kept Philipp's offer in mind, but my priority remained to become a permanent part of the marching band's lead group. I wanted to continue to pay my aggressors. Marian was also one of those who collected protection money from me. He was the one who once told me the story that I would lose my skin color when I washed. I kept hoping that the people who tormented me would eventually receive their rightful punishment. When it came to finding new insults for me, Marian remained by far the most diligent. Because I grew darker in the summer, he would insult me as a darkie-n*****. In winter I became lighter again and they called me eskimo-n*****. I was "pulled through the cocoa too long" (which is a German proverb meaning to pull somebody's leg), or should not always see everything "so black". If I went to Nuremberg with the commuter train, I was, even with ticket, a "Schwarzfahrer" (= "black passenger", i.e. a fare dodger). The people who insulted me were amused by every insult, as if they had just invented it very creatively. It just didn't stop and weighed heavily on me. I had known racist phrases for quite some time by now. Each new insult against me was an additional drop for my barrel of rage.

In the marching band I had made it. I was finally allowed to march in the parades. My youngest uncle was the baton leader from time to time and also led practice sessions. One day I wasn't even safe during one of these rehearsals: racism caught up with me here, too, and developed a cruel group dynamic. Robert was a member of the local wind band and played the trumpet. He was not the brightest, but had always left me alone for the most part. Until that day, when my uncle led the practice session and called a break for all of us. He left the room and I waited for Olaf and Heiner, my two friends from the group. Then Robert suddenly said loudly " Briquet, come here! Now come here briquet, I'm cold and I'll light you up a little." I did not know where to turn. To my absolute dismay, many laughed, even my buddy Olaf, who was standing next to Robert. Heiner didn't notice anything and continued chatting with Christiane. I was not only disappointed, I was outraged. Nevertheless, I smiled sheepishly. The laughter of the others spurred Robert on. Again and again he called me "briquette." He just didn't stop until my uncle came back and resolutely told Robert to shut up immediately. If Niko, Marion, Ralph or Kerstin had been there, they would have supported me and put an end to all this. But as it was, I was pretty much on my own and had reached a turning point. I had finally had enough of all this racist filth that littered my life. That's why I started skipping practice classes and researched more and more about martial arts. To do this, I went to the library of the city of Lauf. A friendly and understanding woman worked there, and one day I asked her about Black literature. She spent a moment searching and gave me a book by Martin Luther King Jr. It contained German translations of his sermons and speeches. I checked the book out for a week and returned it unread. I was not ready for it.

In the summer of 1987, we traveled to Greece for the third time. In previous years, the car trip from the city of Lauf to Thessaloniki took a whole day and a half. This year we did it differently and got on a plane. At Nuremberg airport I discovered her for the first time: Carmen. She was a tall girl with long blond curls, a pout and sparkling blue eyes. She lived in an area of the city of Lauf that I only passed through on my way to the marching band. I had nothing to do with the people there. Now Carmen was squatting on a luggage cart and had a face as long as a fiddle. Apparently she didn't feel like going on vacation with her parents. A short time later, however, I lost sight of Carmen. It was no wonder, because with uncles and aunts we were a total of three families and there was quite a hustle and bustle. Besides, we were standing at another ticket counter. What I could not know at the time, of course: A few years later, the beautiful blonde girl became my first great love and witness to an unspeakably bad experience. I liked Greece. I liked the hospitality, the weather and especially the sea. I fished a lot or went snorkeling equipped with a trident to poke underwater holes for octopus. I enjoyed the two weeks and recharged my batteries for the coming school year, as I made the transition to junior high school.

This was a real new beginning for me. The school was on the other side of town and I had to take the bus there. I was pretty sure that the kids would be much smarter now and would therefore not spew out any dull, racist slogans. And sure enough, that's what happened. At the junior high school, Melvin and I were the only non-*white* kids in the class, because the Turkish kids were ghettoized into "tü" classes. There were, for example, the 3a, b, c and also the 3tü. This segregation continued up to and including the ninth grade. So everything was different at the junior high school. I made friends with Richie, the Greek. Together we had a lot of fun and did many stupid things. He was a real friend with whom I went through thick and thin. Things didn't go so well in seventh grade history class. On the subject of colonialism, my teacher talked about how the "lower n***** tribes were able to participate in the world economy with the help of the colonizers and thus become civilized." All eyes were on me. I was ashamed of the history teacher's claim and looked down at the ground. I would have preferred to sink into the ground. In one swoop, my dream of being an accepted part of the class had been shattered. My back was against the wall. Thoughts shot through my guts like lightning. Should I do nothing, defend myself, or jump up and run out of the classroom? There it was again, that unspeakable, insatiable rage. Tears welled up in my eyes and I ran out. In the restroom, I let all my inner frustration run free and pounded my fists against the tile wall. After I had vented, I returned to class and sat down in my seat to the concerned looks of my classmates. Richie was not there that day and because he was my bench neighbor, I sat alone. After class, the teacher called me over, waited until everyone left the classroom, and then began to put his statements into perspective. He said that the curriculum called for original language, because that would give a historically accurate account of the circumstances. I shouldn't make such a fuss, because he didn't mean it that way, and anyway, he also had "colored" acquaintances. I asked him where they lived. My teacher blamed me. He had held out his hand to me in a friendly manner, and I had slapped it aside. Apparently, I did not want to understand the conflict between good teaching and old-fashioned words. My soul caught fire. I was exposed to racism helplessly and no one cared.

I was profoundly sad all the time. Olaf also went to junior high school with me, but we had almost no contact anymore. My former best buddy was two grades above me and there was nothing left of our former friendship. Luckily I had Richie. He was my age, we had the same sense of humor and he was my new best friend. Nevertheless, things were not going well at school. Contrary to my parents' expectations, I had a hard time. I had trouble concentrating and, at 13 years old, my mind kept wandering. And then I went to martial arts training for the first time. I wanted to become a real martial arts champion. I did a lot to make that happen. I kept skipping my music practice sessions. My excuses got wilder and wilder so that I could skip the practice sessions with Mr. Lehmwand and go to the self-defense classes. I was still active in the marching band, but after the incident with Robert, I didn't feel as safe here as I used to. I was having much less fun. Instead I visited another TSV karate course given by Jürgen Mayer as well. So I could keep it a secret that I was attending a self-defense course. Mr. Lehmwald apparently had hardly any contact with the people from the marching band and so my missing hours were not noticed at all. Since we played the same songs and marches anyway, I didn't need to practice much.

At home there was more and more of a crisis. I was a latchkey kid and the fact that I was hanging around after school was hardly ever noticed. Once I forged my father Eduard's signature to cover up an F. Of course, my attempt at forgery was discovered and the school wrote a letter to my parents, but I intercepted that, too. At the next parent-teacher conference, everything came out and an angry M. came home and yelled at me. Our relationship continued to cool noticeably since 1987. M. had a narcissistic personality, which she cloaked behind egoism. I instinctively recognized that something was wrong and increasingly separated myself. M. thought I was stealing money to buy things. In truth, I was stealing the money to pay the gang that continued to oppress me. I just wanted to remain unharmed. My thefts made M. sad and angry. I couldn't help it, and I didn't skip any trouble. I didn't have a driver's license, but I drove around on a moped. Promptly the police caught me. When the letter from the court came, I felt uneasy. I didn't really think my offense was bad. After all, I only drove around the commuter train parking lot on weekends when there were no cars there. At the same time as the charges were filed, a letter from the juvenile court came. M. made an appointment and we met a friendly officer there. The woman asked about my family background, father and mother, school and hobbies. She also asked if I would like to know who my real father was. But before I could think and answer, M. intervened with a clear and definite

"No, we don't!". Her face was petrified. The juvenile court worker took her notes and we left the office. I was lucky, a few weeks later the case was dropped. But one thing remained and had even grown: my curiosity about the Black part in me. M. remained as secretive about this as ever. That's why I turned to Hildegard, my grandmother's sister. She had had a new, Black Army boyfriend for a few weeks, was full of happiness and was quite forthcoming in my matter. Hildegard was a small, petite woman in her mid-50's. Her boyfriend of the same age was very tall and sturdily built. One afternoon I met Hildegard in front of her front door, which was right in the house next to my great-grandmother. I looked at her and asked her very directly if she knew who my genitor was. She answered just as spontaneously that she knew him by sight, that his name was Paul J. and that he had been a member of the military police in the army barracks in the city of Fürth from 1974 to 1975. I was flabbergasted. I asked a few more questions, but got no more usable answers. So I went home with new knowledge. I didn't have African roots, but African-American roots. That changed my entire world view. I did not talk about it with my parents. But M. quickly got wind of my questioning. When I came home a few evenings later, M. was waiting on the couch in the living room, staring angrily at me. Furiously, she blurted out, "You are nothing, you have nothing, and you will always be nothing!" I reacted aggressively and demanded that she just leave me alone. She called me names and insinuated that I had bought a new sweatshirt with stolen money. As proof, she presented me with a sweater that I had bought together with her three months ago. The alcohol had probably not missed its effect. I was taken aback, but replied even more aggressively what she wanted from me. Then she said that she knew exactly what I was up to. I was still clueless. All I knew was that Eduard was working the late shift and wouldn't be home until 10 p.m. I had no idea what I was up to. There were still three hours to go. All this time I hadn't looked M. in the face, but now our eyes met. Her eyes were glassy and her speech slurred. M. was at her best. She didn't know what to do with me anymore, I was always making trouble. Then it dawned on me what it was all about. She had heard about my conversation with Hildegard through Grandma. I yelled at her that she wouldn't know what I had to go through so far in this shitty life and that she couldn't understand it either because she was *white* and was making a secret of my Black identity. Then she started again with this "You have nothing and you are nothing" talk and I was already on my way out of the living room, upstairs to my bedroom. As I stood at the door, she said in a calm and monotone voice, "You are the result of rape. That's why you don't need to know anything about your genitor." I didn't know where to put myself. What was this right now? Me, the result of sexual abuse? I felt sick to my stomach. I went to my room without a word and didn't come out all evening. This revelation from M. threw my life over the edge. I cried all evening and went through every emotion possible: despair, anger, sadness, astonishment, and above all, confused incomprehension. How could anyone say such a thing to a 13-year-old teenager? How could she hide such a terrible thing from me for so long? What had to be going on inside M. when she looked at me? Where should I go? Who could I talk to about it? All these questions found no answers.

The next day I did not go to school, which nobody at home noticed. I was walking like a ghost and just hated everything I saw, including myself once again. A single question ran through my mind non-stop, "What will become of me if I have genes like this?" This question preoccupied me so much that I distanced myself from everything that was dear and right to me. I changed massively. Until then, I had mostly been a naive boy, but now I was deadly serious, impulsive and angry. I was torn between thoughts of anger and reproaches. What must M. feel in the face of her own son? How could she stand to be in a household with me? Suddenly I could understand why it had been so difficult for her to fully accept me as a child. Suddenly her ambivalent nature was explained. At times she was funny and shortly thereafter angry towards me. But then I mourned for myself. Why did she put such an emotional burden on her 13-year-old son? Why was she so cruel and numb? Why didn't she protect me? I was completely desperate. I was falling behind in school and I was only doing nonsense. In my head I was obsessively preoccupied with one thing: "These thoughts must disappear, they are destroying me."

I was on the verge of insanity and if I hadn't had Richie, I would have broken. He had no idea what was going on behind closed doors with us, but he was an important distraction for me. Our honest friendship continues to this day. Every time I think of how lucky I was with him, tears run down my face. Thank you, my dear friend, you saved me and without even knowing it.

Richie and I also got into some mischief. Somehow I came

into possession of a gas pistol and one evening we both walked from downtown Lauf to my house. We crossed the Lauf bridge, which crosses the Pegnitz river from the city center to the left side of the city of Lauf. When we were at the foot of the bridge, we turned around. I took the gas pistol out of my jacket pocket, pointed it at the supposedly deserted bridge and pulled the trigger. It went off with a loud bang. We were startled, as no one expected it to still be working. The shock was followed by childish laughter until we saw blue light. Instinctively, we ran, split up and hid. I dashed to the Pegnitzwiese, a large green area that runs along the river Pegnitz. On the riverbank, I disguised myself behind bushes and loose barbed wire. The police car drove onto the lawn – and slowly towards me. An officer held out a flashlight and shone it around. I squeezed down and didn't move an inch. Then the cone of light came closer and closer to me. My breath caught in my throat. It stopped and I thought I was screwed. Fortunately, I must have been hidden so well that he overlooked me. I waited for quite some time before I dared to come out of hiding. I ran across the field and straight home. My father intercepted me in the hallway and tried to interrogate me. I told him that nothing had happened. But Eduard was skeptical, because Richie had arrived at our row house a few minutes before me and had inquired in a panic whether I was there. When I arrived a few moments after him, my dad was already suspicious. Nevertheless, our little Richie-Tibor secret has not come to light until today. By the way, there was a reason why the cops were chasing us with blue lights. At the moment when I drew the gas pistol, the well known homeless Rainer came out of a tiny alley on the other side of the bridge. He was once again drunk to the limit and staggering toward the small bridge. When I pulled the trigger and a shot was fired, Rainer was so startled that he fell over backwards. This fall was observed by the patrol who were routinely on the opposite alley. The officers assumed that a capital crime had occurred right before their eyes and immediately took up pursuit. They followed me, the alleged shooter, to the Pegnitzwiese and waited for reinforcements. A second patrol finally drove to the "crime scene" and eventually gave the all-clear, as the alleged corpse got up again and staggered in the direction of the sleeping area in the meadow. A few days later I read about it in the newspaper "Laufer Pegnitzzeitung" and was amused by it. But immediately I felt ashamed and doubted my nature. How could I be happy about something so despicable? Poor Rainer. . . . That's how it had constantly been with me since the ruthless revelation of M.. It was as if angels and demons were sitting on my shoulders, feeding me their opinions and instigating me to action.

I decided to give the marching band another chance and to develop my skills in martial arts. I didn't see any light at the end of the tunnel in junior high school, but somehow I managed to pass the seventh grade. My elementary and secondary school friends lived in the same area as I did, but we went our separate ways. Sometimes we still saw each other and had short chats, but they became less and less frequent. During the summer vacations I was almost only out and about and avoided M. as much as I could. I was still deeply hurt and simply couldn't deal with the way she had told me about my origins.

In the late summer of 1989, eighth grade began. I sat next to

Richie again and we fancied a young, attractive teacher. I didn't get much out of class. The lessons were either boring as hell or infuriating. History lessons were sometimes about the "great explorers" and the colonization of Africa. When historical untruths were repeated, I sometimes objected, but often I said nothing and instead just got upset silently. I was surprised that there was not a single mention of National Socialism. Apparently, Bavaria's ministers of education had no idea and thought that teenagers should not be bothered to learn about Nazis. However, they did not vanish into thin air after the war or wake up in 1945 with new, philanthropic thoughts and were freed from their evil worldview. Instead, they hid from the Allies in farms and attics, obtained false passports, and continued to live peacefully in the face of the Nuremberg trials. They had children and fed them their racist poison. And so one thing led to another. Now young Nazis were among us, directing their hatred toward minorities and people with different opinions. I stood for both and much more. Since I now had changed my vita from an African to half an African-American, I also represented the occupier for some right-wing individuals. They were happy to let me feel that. The worst evenings were the church fairs and old town festivals, when the alcohol flowed in streams and loosened the right-wing tongue. There I was then at best the "Laffer Ni**erla", inspired by the "Laffer Bimbela" (a sloppy bon vivant from an old poem). I was also called n*****, bimbo (i.e. darkie), or monkey boy by the more impudent people. The very funny ones among the *whites* kept calling me Sarotti Mohr (i.e. "Sarotti blackamoor", the mascot of a Berlin chocolate company) or just Mohr. It was unbearable for me and at the first opportunity I went home to my room and was brooding. A new question was added to the others, "Why was I born into such a world?". People, just like children, can be inconsiderately cruel when old thought patterns are recalled in them. I was 14 years old and wanted to run away, only I didn't know where to go. I was getting worse and worse at school, so the air was thick at home. With my impulsive nature, I stirred up the trouble even more. I lost my nerves around M., quickly freaked out and became loud so that she would leave me alone. I could not build up real trust with any person. My solitary nature from childhood had long since become manifest. What insults I had experienced as a boy kept flaring up in my being. I obsessively assumed that sooner or later every *white* person would offend me or throw stupid insults at me. I was infinitely tired of sayings like "I don't mean any harm" or "Everyone says that and it's not so bad." I called these comments "racistisms." The most annoying defense of these racist comments for me was: "I can't help it if that's what they say!" This response was most often hurled at me when, for example, I was upset that N****kuss (German pejorative term for a small chocolate-covered cake filled with foamy sugar) was being said and everyone was staring at me, waiting for me to respond.

Racist language often survives many generations. In each person who uses this language, the words have their own effect – racism has an individual quality. Even if the speakers are not necessarily being intentional, the language, phrases, and their historical contexts remain racist. Things hurt, and even if they are supposedly said only unconsciously, they can affect people profoundly. It is actually quite simple: Anyone who ignores any criticism and still uses words like Z*schnitzel (i.e. "gipsy schnitzel") or N****kuss is clearly expressing an attitude and outlook on life with their vocabulary. Whoever utters these words approvingly accepts that people will be hurt and ignores racist structures. And anyone who doesn't know what one is "allowed to say anymore" so that people of a different skin color, origin or sexual orientation don't feel insulted or humiliated has simply never asked them.

5. A job for Blacks

In 1990, the year of the fall of the Berlin Wall, my relationship with M. improved. Suddenly I was no longer the focus of my environment, because there was a new minority in the area, and Germans who had relocated to the area were now the enemies. I, on the other hand, did what everyone in my peer group did and watched cool hip-hop videos. Out of the blue, I was popular, even with the girls from the neighboring high school. We met at the bus stop in front of the Bitterbachhalle. This hall was our sports facility and since school buses went in all directions from there, this was a central gathering point for the high school students. One girl in particular caught my eye. She was taller than the others, had straight blonde hair and an open, friendly manner. Her name was Heike and we became close in the spring of '91. We quickly got along well and one day we kissed for the first time. I was happy. Heike took me almost everywhere and introduced me to her friends. I didn't really belong in the intellectual clique of high school students – but they respected me. A few times I visited Heike at home and her mother was very open-minded and friendly to me. I had problems with her father. At first I thought he was afraid I would "mess up" his only daughter. But the reason for his rejection became clear very quickly. He didn't like me because of my skin color. I, however, had a compulsive need to want to please everybody, and Heike's father's rejection was a bitter slap in the face for me. I tried to reason for a while, "I was born and raised in the city of Lauf, after all. The only thing that distinguishes me from the other teenagers is the color of my skin. How can one reject a person because of that?" But I achieved nothing with that. Heike made up for all the negative with her good humor and light-hearted manner. We spent a wonderful spring and summer together, went to the open-air swimming pool in the city of Lauf a few times, or feasted on an ice cream sundae at Campo Eis on the Lauf market square. It felt good with her. I spent the first three weeks of summer vacation with my parents in Greece again. When we came back, things between Heike and me were not like before. She broke up with me.

I retreated back into my shell. I didn't make it into the ninth grade, and I had to repeat the eighth grade. Among all the former seventh graders who were younger than me, I missed Richie immensely. To me, my new classmates were kids I didn't warm up to. I had the same teachers, so classes were still boring. I came to the conclusion that school just wasn't for me. So I became extra lazy again and already after the first semester I was in danger to fail again and then to be kicked out of the junior high school. My parents wanted to prevent this and sent me to private lessons. Now I sat there two afternoons a week and a young math student tutored me. The problem was not my lack of mathematical talent, I was not too stupid. I just didn't want to study. I was being lost in the German education system. Nothing linked me to school. My everyday life there was too much dominated by racist insults, history books that only told the *white* perspective of colonization, and teachers who had no hesitations in saying the n-word. I often longed for the Tü class because the students there received lessons from Turkish teachers. Turkish culture was also on the curriculum. I myself continued to struggle with myself. For so many years I didn't know which culture I belonged to and didn't know which language belonged to me. German or English. Some people asked me if I experienced xenophobic attacks often. Their pity reinforced my lack of identity. I often heard the word "xenophobic" in connection with racism – as well as in the media. I was a German Black teenager and I had no contact with other Black people, let alone a Black German community. If people called me "foreign," it was clear to me I didn't belong anywhere. So I was a lonely, angry, Black teenager. In most *white* people around me, I saw potential racists. The only exceptions were my friends from the marching band, Nico, Marion, Ralph, Kerstin and some school friends like Stefan, Tanja and Richie. But I did not trust the adult population of the city of Lauf. I never left any doubt about being the dear and nice Tibor, but inside me anger was boiling. As a 16-year-old I was already over 5.9 feet tall. That's why my teachers continued to dig prejudices out of the relic box in class. While my primary school teacher still thought I could speak perfect English, I was now a regular focus of attention during sports. When basketball was on the schedule, everyone fought over me. But I wasn't good at it at all. I was a martial artist and could jump high, but that alone didn't make me a basketball player. When I repeatedly missed the basket, everyone comforted me by saying that I must be having a bad day. This happened in almost every game. Sometimes I was lucky and hit a few baskets. And although I made no secret of the fact that I had little to do with basketball, I was considered the top favorite in the class. I couldn't handle that at all. This schizophrenia bothered me a lot. At such times, I would take refuge in the library. I dared to try again and told the nice clerk there that I still had a great interest in Black culture and how much it bothered me to be pinned down to any roles. She understood me immediately and recommended the book "Stereotypes and Human Behavior" by Adam Schaff. It was difficult reading, but somehow I understood much better what I was experiencing. Still, there was a huge difference between the theory and reality. I learned that life shows you new facets when you know about the scientific aspects. Still, it just didn't stop striking me inside when I was called n*****, bimbo (i.e. darkie), Arab, or whatever. I started skipping practice sessions with Mr. Lehmwand more often again and changed martial arts groups. We now met outside. In all kinds of weather we fought until one of us was down. I was very agile, fast and strong. That's why I got away with few bruises, at most I suffered a bruised rib or pain in my back. I worked out hard and relentlessly, unnoticed by almost everyone. Richie got an idea of my skills when I was able to get him out of a hairy situation. But we never talked about it any further. I had learned to keep a lot of frustration and sadness inside and thus closed myself off from the outside world.

Through music videos, CDs and reports in the teen magazine Bravo, rappers like Ice-T and Public Enemy became stars, and many casual acquaintances saw the cool hip-hop lifestyle in me. Also, some girls were dying to have a Black boyfriend. I even got offers from older girls, which I gratefully accepted. We sometimes met in the afternoons or at weekends. Two of them were even allowed to drive cars and I was happy to be driven around. I could have gone on like this forever.

One day my youngest uncle took me to squash. I stuck with it and practiced regularly. When I had nothing to do during the weekends, my martial arts group would go to a field in Nuremberg. There we fought against other groups. The first time I joined, I immediately wanted to participate. This martial clash, the shouting and the fairness – all this encouraged me to try it myself two weeks later. I was in top shape and, as always, a huge fury was raging in my belly. When we arrived, there were already 15 or 20 people outside the lawn. I was startled for a moment when I discovered a familiar face in among them: Gustav, the Nazi, who had threatened me as an elementary school student. He recognized me, too. Somehow he looked frail and tired. We lined up across from each other and with a clap we were off. Gustav stormed towards me with a determined face. I was full of adrenaline. His right shoulder twitched, I dove quickly and he launched his right haymaker into nothingness. As I rose from cover, I gave him two short punches in the ribs with my left. He cried out and lowered his defenses so I gave him a straight fist right on the chin. He fell over like a house of cards. I obviously landed a lucky punch. There was this nasty guy now lying in front of me with his tongue hanging out. Standing over him like that gave me an incredible feeling of happiness. Suddenly I felt pride and a joy that I had missed for so long. I turned around and was able to dodge the blow of a new attacker just in time. He was about 5.5 feet tall. A wiry guy who, like most, was dressed all in black. Judging by his movements, he was a jiu-jitsu fighter, which I appreciated. He hit me a few times and I hit him as well, it was an even fight. Then he caught me below the solar plexus and it was like a switch was flipped in me. I raged, got a hold of him, lifted him up and just dropped him. When he got back up, my punch frequency was twice as fast as his and he went down on his knees and finally to the ground under the force applied. I was done with him and ran to the car. There I waited a few minutes until the others arrived and we left. We stopped briefly at the fast food joint for refreshments. The group of opposing fighters passed us on the bus. The guy I took down after Gustav pointed his finger at me and said something to the people on the bus that I couldn't understand. He gave me a dirty grin and I looked away, not thinking anything more of it.

When I got back home to my room, I wondered about how things were going to go in my life. I was quite aware that girls only wanted to be seen with me because of a trend and choose me as a partner. This phase would pass and then I would be written off again. Before it got to that point, I preferred to end these stories myself right away. I managed the eighth grade only by the skin of my teeth. That's why it didn't make sense to stay at the junior high school. Robert, the part-time racist from the marching band, got wind of my school problems. One Friday after practice, he chatted me up with a heavy alcoholic buzz. We were standing at the urinal in the men's room and Robert was grinning arrogantly. He said that since we were already here, he had the perfect job for me. I should, like most of my bimbo (i.e.

darkie) friends, just become a restroom attendant. "There's real dough for your mud hut, and if you're diligent, you might even be able to move into a wooden hut with your ten kids," he agitated. I looked at him pityingly and left the toilet without saying anything. But this time I did not hold back my anger. I slipped out of the TSV Lauf gym building into the parking lot in front of the restaurant. I looked for Robert's old car. I fiddled with his rear right tire with the toothpick of my Swiss Army knife until it hissed. Robert sat in the pub and continued to get drunk. In the end he was so drunk that he was driven home once again. It wasn't until the next afternoon that he came by to pick up his car. I was playing with a friend at the miniature golf course across the street and had a good view of the parking lot. Robert got behind the wheel, hungover. He awkwardly started the clunker and drove off. To get off the TSV grounds, he had to climb a hill. He drove up this hill with a flat rear tire, only to stop at the next street. Angrily he ran around his vehicle and ranted and raved. Little demon and little angel on my shoulder argued for a while. The moralist in me criticized me for messing with other people's property. I didn't see Robert anymore, but his cursing could be heard for several yards. In the end, all he had to do was plug the valve back in and pump air into the tire. So I didn't cause any permanent damage. Thus I did not have a bad conscience for long and the demon won. Playing tricks on my opponents undetected was a very good feeling and I enjoyed the satisfaction to the fullest.

As for school, my parents did not waste much time and enrolled me in a private school. I should get a good degree, no matter what the cost. However, before I went to school in a foreign city, I had to take care of one more matter. I had a score to settle with the oppressors of my childhood. Those brutes who had tormented, insulted, spat at and kicked me were going to get what they deserved. At a favorable moment, I first intercepted Marian. Suddenly I was standing in front of him. By now I was a head taller than him and asked him what he was going to call me now. I scrutinized him from above and realized how much the alcohol had destroyed him in the last two years. By his drinking, then, he had done my work himself. Wordlessly, I left him standing there and walked away.

I spent the time until the summer vacations gambling with my SEGA Megadrive. I waited anxiously for the new school in another city. And then, during the vacations, I experienced a new chapter of racism for me: racial profiling. Of course, I didn't know this term at that time. But I quickly learned that for the Bavarian police it was enough to have a dark skin color and to be male to be a potentially suspicious and dangerous person. In the meantime, I had long since obtained a moped driver's license and enjoyed riding around on the little motorbike. A policeman had it in for me. As soon as he saw me, I was stopped and checked. But that was only the beginning of an odyssey and many encounters with the police. As a 6.2 feet tall 16-year-old with Black skin, I was the usual suspect for all sorts of things. I was relatively well known in the town of Lauf. I greeted everyone and made small talk with most people, so I was actually quite popular. But since a couple of months there was a policeman at the police station who obviously had a problem with me. The first time we met, I had just come from school and was on my way home. I got off the bus and crossed Altdorfer Street at the gas station. Out of the corner of my eye I noticed a car turning on the street. I turned into Niebelungen Street and bang, a police car stopped right next to me. I didn't mind and strolled on. I didn't get far, however, because the officer got out of the car and shouted, "Freeze." I looked around and realized he meant me, so I took a few steps back to the patrol car and asked if anything was up. He replied that it was a routine check. I was to tell where I was coming from at this hour and what was in my briefcase. Yes, I had a black diplomatic briefcase as a knapsack. It was covered with many stickers. I replied that I was coming from school and of course there were school supplies in the briefcase. It was shortly after 11:30. We had to leave school early because one lesson was cancelled due to a teacher's conference regarding the annual report cards. Besides, one didn't do much three days before the end of the school year. The officer asked me quite directly if I had ever had anything to do with the police. I answered in the affirmative because of the dismissed case for driving without a license. The next question was whether I had anything to do with drugs. There I had to laugh out loud. "I am an athlete and have never drunk alcohol in my life, let alone smoked," I stated. I could tell by the look on his face that he didn't believe me. "Carefully put the case on the hood and open it," he ordered me. I still thought it was funny, since I had nothing to blame myself for. As I popped the latch, his younger colleague pushed me aside. The leader, in his late 30s or so, had three green stars on his shoulder and the younger policeman, in his mid-20s or so, had two. Immediately Three-Star set to work on the case, searching it, and when he had emptied the pencil case, he told his young colleague that the disguises of the

Africans were getting better and better. He should pat me down. That's when I stopped laughing. In the meantime, about five elderly women were staring out of their windows, curiously observing the scene. Starting from my shoulders, the policeman patted me down. Through my exercises in the martial arts groups, I had learned to control anger. It could only be seen in my face. An elderly woman I knew well happened to pass by the incident and stopped, puzzled. She immediately started ranting and walked up to Three-Star. "Listen, that' s Tibor! What is he supposed to have done that you treat him like a felon?" Three-Star replied that she should please move on and not disturb the police operation. Mrs. Bensel, that was her name, was my great-grandmother's neighbor and she had known me since I was born. She was visibly not amused and threatened to call the head of the department if she was not told immediately what I had done. This had an effect. Three-Star went to her and explained something that I could not hear. Thereupon Mrs. Bensel became even more energetic and said that I was not an African drug courier, but Tibor. Three-Star gave Two-Star a hand gesture, whereupon he let go of me. I went to the hood, closed my suitcase, and was about to leave the scene when the older policeman called me over and warned me, "We know what kind of guy you are, and we've got our eyes on you from now on, Mr. Sturm." With an angry face, I trudged home. Mrs. Bensel said something else to me, but I was like in a tunnel and heard nothing more. When I arrived home, no one was there. I was glad of that, because it gave me time to vent my anger on the cushions in the living room. I screamed the anger out of me. When I was done, I lay down, completely exhausted, and took a nap. As soon as I dozed off, I startled up with a thought:

"How did Three-Star know my last name?" In my mind, I went through every moment of the police operation again. Neither I, nor Mrs. Bensel had mentioned my last name. Nor did I have any identification with me. What was this conspiracy against me? The uncertainty drove me crazy. I didn't dare talk to anyone about it. Who was going to believe me that the police were trying to frame me. I never felt more helpless in my Black skin. I had never been in more trouble because of it than I was now. I was to find out a few months later why I was so caught in the crosshairs.

6. Black man's revenge

In the late summer of 1991, my performance at the new school improved dramatically. The reason was obvious to me. I no longer was the only non-*white*, and in class we used various issues from other cultures as examples for German principles. Mathematics originated with the Pharaohs and the first human came from Africa. In history class, it was doubted that Jesus was a *white* man. After all, he had been born and raised in North Africa. It is hard to believe that his mother Mary was not Black at that time. I liked these theories because they helped me feel more comfortable being me. My self-esteem was improving. However, I understood the behavior of *white*, German people less and less.

During our obligatory three-week vacation in Greece, I noticed a German family in our regular restaurant, Stavros. I had never seen them in our resort of Neo Peramos. They were probably there for the first time, but immediately left a lasting impression. The woman complained loudly that there was no "Wiener Schnitzel" and no other German dish. The man agreed with her and the weird gestures of the two children reminded me of Louis de Funès. I had a fit of laughter, drawing attention to myself. My stomach hurt so much that I left the restaurant to catch my breath. The nagging family left without having ordered anything. Already at that time I was wondering why many Germans are so dissatisfied all together.

The lessons in the new school were fun and I found a new friend in H.L.W. and he is still a friend today. He was a vegetarian and that was a whole new world for me. He also constantly enthused about Jamaica and infected me with his wanderlust. Along with my better grades, my relationship with M. also improved. One fall weekend, I happened to meet Teuber, one of the fighters from the group that fought in the field. He told me that the group was sorry for what had happened back then. I had no idea what he meant. He went on to say that an important piece of information was withheld from me at the Nuremberg Field fight. It was about the guy I took down second to Gustav. He was a police officer and obviously a pretty sore loser. Since that day, he had it in for me and wanted to "get back at me." Now it all made sense. All the police checks, the warning of Three-Star, and the rough pat-down of Two-star. I started to panic. What should I do, where could I turn? When I was alone again, I decided to look for allies. I needed a brotherhood. In the city of Lauf, the Turkish citizens lived largely as if in a parallel society. They went to the same schools as everyone else, had ordinary jobs, but I never saw them at church fairs and other celebrations with *whites*. There were exceptions, of course. For example, most of the Turkish classmates were in the low-level secondary school. There were a few in the junior high school and very few in grammar school. For the *white* majority population, however, these successes were always reason enough to dismiss demands for equal, fair educational opportunities. The unanimous argument was: "Each of you can make it if you set your mind to it and work hard enough." This completely ignored the extent to which young people were discouraged when they were confronted only with *white* perspectives, always and everywhere. Their entire school years were dominated by *white* stories in *white* textbooks. Finding one's own non-*white* identity was therefore extremely difficult. Today, thanks to the Internet, this is different. But in the 80s and early 90s, things were different.

My fear of the police was enormous. So I joined the Turkish youths when I was in the city of Lauf. Actually, I fraternized with Turkish rioters from the ghetto. They were the outlaws who didn't give a shit about anything. As soon as someone crossed them, it went boom. Our relationship was more of a love-hate thing. When we were together, the air was filled with adrenaline and violence. Crazy enough, the Turks called me "Arab" or "Katil" after seeing me in action. Katil means killer.

The marching band played only a tiny secondary role in my life. I took Jiu-Jitsu lessons on three afternoons or roamed the city with H.L.W.. My parents didn't have a clue about it. On the contrary. They thought I was in school until 3:00. That was rarely the case.

The afternoon hours were actually dedicated to doing homework. However, since we usually did this during class, we didn't need to be in the school building and roamed around the city. It was a pretty carefree time for me. I became really good at squash and won many club competitions. One day I met a Black guy in Nuremberg who was as tall as I was and also looked quite similar to me. Raymond was from the city of Fürth. Since my genitor was also stationed in that city, I had to be alert. But my hopes were quickly dashed. Raymond knew his Black father, after all – he still lived in the city of Fürth. Raymond asked me where I played basketball . When I answered that I didn't play basketball, but squash, he was stunned. "Do you know a Black squash pro?" he asked. With a question like that, Raymond set a new process in motion for me – it was a wave of recognition of being Black. He imparted a Black lifestyle to me over the next few months, and I learned that he, too, had similar experiences with arbitrary police stops as I had. I began to become more and more involved with Black History. I read about the unspeakable atrocities of the slave traders and the German conquerors. The picture that had been painted in public school history classes began to crumble more and more. I discovered the numerous traces of colonial history in my surroundings. In Nuremberg, for example, there is still Nettelbeck Street. Joachim Nettelbeck was a slave trader who was first celebrated as a hero by the National Socialists and then in a revisionist way by some history teachers. I was so angry and disappointed. How could one overlook such a terrible fact? How did they treat people with dark skin in the country where I was born? I couldn't stand it and began to rebel against everything *white*. I liked school because of its multiethnicity and I got better and better. In math, I made it from a F to an A straight up. So I graduated in 1993 and returned to the city of Lauf.

Still, I lacked direction in my life. I was restless, seeking both my identity and education. I began training as a chef, but had to end it due to an allergy to flour dust. Then I wanted to become a professional athlete and practiced squash and basketball. My grandmother gave me a lot of money during this time again. I didn't ask where she got it and she didn't ask what I did with it. In the meantime I had a new girlfriend. Ronja was eight years older than me. Anyway, I mostly hung out with older people. But after half a year Ronja was still more of a buddy for me. And so in spring 1994 it was over again between us. The relationship with her showed me once again that I did not allow any closeness. I didn't care about trust – I didn't need it and I didn't give it. People had simply disappointed me too often – exclusively *white* people. When they did offer me their friendship, I let myself get involved, but never let it become too personal and intimate. The scars on my soul were too deep. I was often called insensitive and arrogant – I preferred that to bimbo (i.e. darkie) or n*****.

Raymond's father, who taught me a lot about the diaspora and being Black, warned me. I should never become an angry Black man like the disciples of Black Panther were. The problem was: I was a tall, Black man who was well toned and had experienced racism, oppression, and ignorance in my childhood. This, of course, did not go without consequences. I was a friendly guy but physical closeness made me uncomfortable. That did not fit together. Police checks in the city of Lauf were frequent and I avoided being alone in the small alleys of the city at night. I only felt reasonably safe with the Turkish homeboys. Once I was on my way back from Lauf's Old Town Festival with Melvin, whom I met by chance. As we walked across the bridge late at night, he told me that I was a kind of role model for him.

We had hardly seen each other since elementary school, and angry as I was, I couldn't handle that kind of emotionalism at all. I told him he needed to find another Black role model. I was no good for that. After all, I had no identity myself and was only puting on a strongman act for self-protection. But Melvin didn't hear that at all. For him, the matter was clear: I was good-looking, had girlfriends and even a car. He was too small and too insecure. I kept my mouth shut, but after that evening I avoided Melvin. I just wasn't in the mood for his self-pity. The angel on my left shoulder preached more empathy, but the demon told me to take care of myself and not get hurt again.

In the summer of 1994, I met Carmen again. She was even more beautiful than she had been at the airport umpteen years ago. Six feet tall, light brown, long hair and still this model face. I had inquired about her from acquaintances and learned that she had a boyfriend. I left it at that, because I wanted to get away from the city of Lauf. I moved away and lived in Leipzig, Munich, Frankfurt/Main and Cologne. There I always lived in small shacks and dealt with various theories that were important for my personality development and finding my identity. In Munich I lived in a one-room apartment. I met an old *white* woman, let's call her Vera. She opened my eyes about many things in life. In Munich, by the way, the police tormented me especially often. The checks with pat-downs and the questions "Where are you from?", "Where are you going?" took place daily and sometimes several times a day. I now flinched at every patrol car, which made me suspicious. If I still laughed with friends when we walked down the street in Schwabing, my face changed to a bitter expression as soon as a police car was in sight. I simply couldn't stand it in the Bavarian capital any longer. So much open racism was terrible for me. You have to imagine that a mix drink of beer and Coke was called n***** there. Every drink menu I opened in the old-established pubs had the n-word written on it in big, bold letters. Every time a regular ordered "10 N*****" and everyone laughed afterwards, I wanted to raze the place to the ground. Munich really broke me. That's why I left that place full of bitterness. I was a traveling, angry Black man with no identity. In addition, I still felt this incredible fear that a perpetrator of violence might be lying dormant in me. In fact, there was hardly a day when I didn't think about where I had originated. This knowledge haunted me like an evil spirit.

I was very tall and had a well-trained body. This had advantages: No one tousled my hair foolishly anymore. I towered over most of my fellow men by a head, and I had the self-confidence of a street fighter. That in turn had a magical effect on insecure personalities. If they were around me, I even more embodied the common stereotype of an arrogant Black man.

I wanted to show it to everyone. At times I had a real desire for revenge. For years I had suffered under the tyranny of small-town racists, and now their children and grandchildren were going to pay for it. Basketball training made my movements smooth and fluid, and I danced exceptionally well for my size. But I felt very lonely among all the "bootleg jerks" who were in the club and elsewhere, just hanging out with me to get a woman. My shell was getting harder and harder and I had long since stopped wanting to please everyone. In fact, I didn't care about anything, it was all about me. *White* society was making fun of me, insulting me and mistreating me. Therefore, I went on the counterattack and behaved like a fighter in all situations. By now I had acquired excellent general education. I was interested in politics because I had learned that only that could change things. I couldn't talk about it with my basketball homies, and my friends didn't want to hear about it either, so I turned away from them. In political community groups, I found the forum to discuss the intolerable conditions for Black people. It wasn't enough for me that successful Black people were shown in *white* media as representing only two professions: Basketball players and rappers. In addition, there were only drug dealers or pimps. These were categories that appeared regularly enough in rap songs. But I wanted to see Black people in executive positions, top politics and as ministers. On German TV, Black people and People of Color were either gangsters or marginal characters. Charles Huber was merely the sidekick of a popular *white* TV detective ("Der Alte") and apart from that I saw Günther Kaufmann a couple of times on the TV show "Derrick". However, these shows were designed for a much older audience and didn't appeal to me at all. In Nuremberg there was a Black man whom everyone only called "Kunta Kinte". From him I got the VHS cassette "Juice – City War" with 2pac. I didn't understand why American movies were only about violence, women and drugs when it came to Black people. Nevertheless, I liked the roles of the protagonists better than the entire public television program with its *white* faces and storylines.

As a child, I found it quite harmless when people called me Jim Knopf, a Black character out of a novel from 1960, written by Michael Ende. Now it made me furious. I wanted to get ahead in life, no matter what. That's why I made an effort to get a spot at university. I didn't have a specific goal, I was just restless. The communal political discussions led nowhere, so I started thinking about my professional future again. I trained basketball like a madman, left squash completely aside and wanted to play in the national league. I had a few friends there by now and they lived well, earned a lot and had pretty girlfriends. It probably would have worked out, too, if I hadn't become an obnoxious, hot-blooded Black young man. So I just didn't fit in with the team anymore. I was self-absorbed and constantly launched unnecessary individual moves. I left the team and looked for something new to get recognition and success. I found all that in streetball. Three against three in a confined space – that was just the thing for me. My circle of friends in the city of Fürth included several former G.I.s. They watched one gangster movie after another. At some point, I got bored with the testosterone-fueled behavior, and I withdrew from them and moved back into my parents' house in the city of Lauf. There I encountered conflicts with M. on a daily basis, because I didn't live according to her ideas. I had never fit into the family image. Either I felt tolerated or I was completely unwanted. M. obviously experienced emotional chaos. But that was not my fault or should I seriously suffer for what had happened to her? I could not accept this and therefore I asked my grandmother about the circumstances of my conception. She hesitated and asked for time to think. She could not tell me about it so easily. Since patience was not one of my strong points, I kept bugging her and then got a surprising account of what had happened.

Without going too deep into details – if my grandma had her way, M. was not raped at all. I was simply an "accident."

It pulled the rug out from under me. I didn't dare to open that can of worms in front of M. one more time, and shut myself off. The tensions between us continued to grow in the following months. I kept my head above water with side jobs. I didn't know where to put myself, but in all the mental chaos I found a like-minded person: the German-American Julia. With our relationship we defied the will of our parents. M. disapproved of our love just as Julia's parents did. The latter were typical Texans, as one would imagine them. Their blond, blue-eyed daughter could find any boyfriend in the world – just not a Black one. M. had a problem with every one of my girlfriends anyway. However, that was fine with me. I didn't go on the Greek vacation anymore and spent a summer with Julia and Melvin, with whom I had a little more contact again. I was alone in the terraced house, but avoided parties or anything like that. During the day I worked out and in the evening I went out with friends to clubs and cafes. When we were out and about in the city of Lauf, I noticed that I was no longer being looked at like an exotic character, but like a threat or a stranger. We also went to Nuremberg museums. The looks in the cafés were already strange for me, but the cherry on top were the questions as to whether I was in the right place in the museum. A curator in the Germanic National Museum told me to my face that the exhibitions were not for me, because my people were not exhibited there anywhere. That had been forbidden for years. I knew immediately what the older woman was alluding to: the ethnological shows that the colonialists put on in the 19th and

20th centuries. At that time, Africans were presented as exotic exhibits to gawking *white* onlookers. In the process, Africans were allowed to be groped, pawed, pinched, poked and, among other things, beaten to see if n***** blood was of a different color. I learned from Kunta Kinte about Angelo Soliman, a Black servant of some nobles who made it to fame during his lifetime. When he died, his prepared corpse was exhibited as a savage in the Imperial Natural History Cabinet in Vienna in 1806. I asked the lady in flawless Franconian, the local dialect, whether she had eaten a Nazi for breakfast, my friends laughed, she got upset and I went my way smiling. I loved this kind of confrontation, because none of these peculiar people expected it. Julia and I were the anarchists of our respective parental homes: I rebelled against M., Julia against her father. That connected us more than love. We talked about it. She told me that she didn't care, she just liked Black people and liked me as a person. In the city of Lauf, Julia's choice of men was thus limited to Melvin and me, and her choice fell on me. I, on the other hand, had noticed that the police checks with her at my side went to zero. So our symbiosis was a partnership of convenience. We were not and did not stay together because of our personalities, it was the circumstances. But one evening I asked her what exactly she liked about me. She replied that I was so tall and strong, good-looking and . . . Then nothing more came. So it was all about my appearance, my inner being didn't matter at all. No wonder. What was my inner being anyway? I was a torn young Black man who didn't say a word about the secret of his origin. My resume was anything but German and in a straight line. I was 18 years old and my journey through life so far was full of curves and stones.

I still had so many questions about being Black, but I couldn't turn to anyone with them. There was nowhere I could get adequate answers. My research on Black initiatives came to nothing. As time went by, a new question arose in me that scratched at my self-esteem. It throbbed in my skull, "Am I just my outer Black shell?". At the time, I fulfilled every stereotype of a Black man. I was known well beyond the city limits on the streetball courts, I had a pretty American girlfriend. But I also realized that for many people I was just a fetish. It was a bad feeling that made me trust the *white* people in my life even less than I already did.

Things were so bad with M. that we didn't even say hello to each other when we met on the street. I was used to anxious ladies of all ages changing sides of the street. But the fact that M. also showed her power by ignoring her own flesh and blood on the street made me furious. What was she so disappointed about? She had raised me to be an emotional idiot and now she was wondering about an adult who did emotionally stupid things. I was raised as an insecure Black boy in a *white* world with no information about being Black. As a teenager, I suffered severe emotional shock, leaving me to wander through life as a young adult, disoriented. The abuse and mistreatment of the racist youth gang had an effect since my childhood. I did not feel at home in Germany.

The constitution states that all citizens have the right to choose their place of residence freely. This does not apply to me. How am I supposed to feel like a German citizen? If, for example, I wanted to move to the city of Jamel in Northwest Mecklenburg, because you can pay cheap rents and do great fishing – I couldn't live there, because Jamel is a Nazi village. And this is manifest, in front of the eyes of the entire nation. One extreme, but it shows, people who look or think differently don't always have the free choice in Germany and don't benefit from the constitution wherever they go.

When I was looking for an apartment, I had enormous problems. On the phone everything was all right and I was invited to the tour. Once there, I was looked at in amazement or immediately asked for my ID. When I showed it, they asked me if I was adopted. And then it was always the same: I never got the apartment. Which *white* German applicant for an apartment with a clean credit report ("Schufa") and other proofs had to put up with such a thing? When I was overcome by the blues in the face of such experiences and wanted to talk to Julia about it, nothing came from her. She walked through life right next to me and yet did not see what I experienced every day. She did not notice the poisonous looks of the people. She didn't notice how women looked at me from top to bottom and then frantically grabbed their bags and held them tightly. We had, flatly, nothing more than a typical American, superficial teenage relationship. When I was spared racial incidents, we got along. On other days, my mood was often in the dumps and we avoided each other. Julia and I were together for just under a year, then it ended without drama. We are still in contact today, she lives in the USA, is happily married and still a good buddy. I can count on that. I moved to the city of Fürth to learn more about my origins. This topic still concerns me today, but it was all-encompassing in the 90s. My grandma told me that M. used to go to a certain club on the city limits of Nuremberg and Fürth regularly with girlfriends. I started looking for possible children of M.'s girlfriends, but did not find any. I found distraction from my missing family history in basketball. I trained harder every day. I was often out with Raymond and we had a great time, but still, I was being checked by young police officers when I was in downtown Nuremberg. In the electronics store, the department store detective followed me around, and even at the bookstore, a detective was on my heels. Girlfriends didn't interest me at all at that time. On the outside, I was a likeable, eloquent, well-trained guy who was simultaneously unapproachable and arrogant. I did not allow any deep, intimate togetherness, because the demons had me firmly in their grip. I was afraid. Afraid of myself and of the person who lurked inside me. On the basketball court I was a better team player, but my impulsiveness was feared. Because under the basket I sometimes was running wild and I vented all my frustration. I lived in a small one-room apartment with cockroaches and Heavy Metal neighbors. There I regularly collapsed and was tormented by fears for the future. Being alone was good for me, but the brooding and negative thoughts were a problem. My grandmother was my anchor during this time. She often called me and asked if everything was okay or if she should get something for me. I had a part-time job in a call center and all I wanted from her was more information about my conception. But she didn't know any more. The cloak of silence was again draped over our family secret. My grandma and her sister took it to the grave with so many other secrets.

7. The first love and the first muzzle

In the summer of 1996, I successfully played basketball in the premier league. But since the club could no longer pay me, I had to give notice on my apartment. Forced to do so, I moved back to my parents' house. When I came back to the city of Lauf, I met Carmen while shopping. We began to talk and arranged to meet for coffee occasionally. This went on for several months. In July, we walked across the Pegnitzwiese, sat down on a park bench and talked for a long time about heaven and earth. Then I kissed her. She was visibly surprised, but also agreed, and so we became a couple. What happened to me now was new. I opened up to Carmen from the first day. We talked about racism and although she didn't experience it personally, she had so much empathy that I felt understood for the first time. I really came alive. One day, for example, we spontaneously drove hundreds of kilometers to the city of Bottrop- Kirchhellen to the amusement park Warner Brothers Movie World, only to discover that we couldn't ride any attraction because long lines of people spoiled our fun before it even started. I was still playing basketball in the city of Fürth and was on the search for myself. At the end of July Carmen and I went on vacation to

Italy. I had been to the town of Bibione a few times as a child. We stayed in a hotel on the beach promenade and I had never felt so free and happy. No drama, no posturing, a completely new feeling for me. On the beach, we daydreamed about our future. Our shared vision included a son named Malik. In my mind, he played on the beach and then ran into Carmen's outstretched arms. Such a carefree, honest bond felt not only new, but right. Our vacation turned somewhat fateful when my money was stolen from my bag on the beach. The idiot I was hadn't left it in the hotel room because I thought it was too risky. So I described what had happened to the hotel owner the night before I checked out. He apologized for his country and told me that I could send the money by wire. I was not used to such kindness, of course. I was blown away. On the way back to the city of Lauf we listened to "Illmatic" by NAS. Loudly we sang

"If I ruled the world, I'd free all my sons. Black diamonds and pearls

Could it be, if you could be mine we'd both shine If I ruled the world

Still livin' for today, in these last days and times."

From Bibione to the city of Lauf an der Pegnitz it was only about 300 miles. Nevertheless, we needed almost a whole day for the trip back. I was so busy singing and rapping that I missed the exits and then had to drive across Austria via the Italian countryside. We didn't care at all. The most important thing was that we had each other and our young love.

When we arrived in the city of Lauf and I was back in my

room, the phone rang. The call pulled me back into the dark world once again. A buddy from martial arts times had been trying to reach me for days, but I was on vacation without a care in the world. He told me that the cop from the fight was still looking for me and was now causing real trouble. Before hanging up, he told me that I could always count on the old crew to take care of me. I had a sinking feeling in my stomach. The next day I talked to the Turkish guys about the case and they also promised to keep their eyes and ears open. I had a Siemens cell phone, so I was reachable by cell phone. As I had been taught in the family, I put up a brave front. I didn't tell Carmen about my problems, because I didn't want to drag her into this. Of course, I didn't succeed very well. I had damn bad days, with the beginnings of paranoid tendencies. Any vehicle that remotely resembled a police car made me cringe. I had been having problems with the club for years, only now they had taken on a new quality. After all, a Nazi cop had it in for me with his vendetta. In retrospect, I found out that that weekend on the field, all the opposing fighters had a right-wing attitude. It was obvious, how else could Gustav have ended up there? I was not surprised that there were policemen present as well. If you are right-wing extremist or national socialist in your mind, you don't change that thinking just because you put on a uniform. I, too, took the Bavarian police entrance exam – and passed. Not a single test question dealt with a possible extremist mindset of the applicant. I would have expected that an entrance exam for police officers would use questioning techniques that could expose liars. Wrong. Instead, I had to write a dictation in which "difficult" words like "venetian blinds" were asked. I was reconsidering my career as a Black police officer when I ran into one of my future instructors. That was in 1992, and he told me that I had no business being here – at the training center for riot police. During an exercise that required us to lie on our stomachs and stand up quickly, he said that terrorists would have no problem hitting me, or rather my Black butt. The aspiring police officers who were lying around me all laughed out loud. I got the invitation to start training and just didn't go.

Racism is not logical, Harry Belafonte once told me. I met him once through his daughter Gina, whom I happened to know. Harry taught me more than any other Black person in my life. His stories about different issues showed me that if you want to make great things happen, it's worth holding on to your opinions and ideals. For example, even as host of the Tonight Show, he had interviewed Robert F. Kennedy. The latter had good contacts with the Justice Department and in 1958 had the idea that the U.S. government should send a sympathetic message in view of the peaceful protests in Birmingham. In the wake of the protests, segregation had been eliminated at many universities. Harry immediately came up with a suggestion. Only a year earlier, he had been to Africa for the first time. What he saw there were hunger and poverty but also a remarkable level of education of many Africans. So Harry suggested to Robert F. Kennedy that the government should support Africans with scholarships. Thus, about 60 African students came to the United States in the winter of 1958/1959. One student enrolled at the University of Hawaii. His name was Barack Hussein Obama Senior. The rest is history. When you are involved in significant historical events in that way, your actions are proven right. Harry Belafonte also told me how Dr. Martin Luther King Jr. called him on many Saturdays months before the March on Washington, D.C. He said he had a lot of work to do. The activist was very aware of the importance of his upcoming speech. Dr. King threw up several times and had no idea how to frame the speech. Through phone calls to friends and allies, "I Have a Dream" emerged. That's how powerful a community can be on something that impacts generations.

I searched for a community for a long time and found ISD, the Initiative of Black People in Germany. It offers a clear structure and an annual federal meeting – only for Black people. On the other hand, there were critical voices that were outraged about the exclusion of *white* partners. That is fundamentally wrong. There are issues that we have to discuss among ourselves because they are understood and empathized with here. Our *white* partners can be interested in the day-to-day racism in our lives, can empathize with situations. But in order to process the severity of these experiences, it takes understanding from other Black people.

Back to the hairy situation involving the streetfighting cop. I was looking for ways to process my inner turmoil, anger and fear. That's how I came up with writing hip-hop lyrics. I had talent and finally found an outlet for my emotions. It was a better way to deal with the constant pressure. Many people were tugging at my future, wanting only what they thought was best for me. But all I wanted to do was make music and play basketball. Since these were no professions for the small-town people around me, they tried to work on me. There was only one family member who empowered me and supported my goals: my dad, Eduard. He told me to go for it. And I did. I wrote hip-hop songs about the things I was experiencing that were bothering me. I drove hundreds of miles to perform in youth centers in front of three random listeners. I performed from Berlin to Backnang in empty halls, full dance halls or at an outdoor youth concert. The effort was to pay off and I got a record contract with a small label from Hannover. In the city of Lauf I recovered from my performances and Carmen was with me. I was carefree and blissful like never before in my life. We went to clubs and just showed up together everywhere. We were popular with our friends and were well-liked. On Saturdays we regularly went to the disco "Trend". It was in Postbauer-Heng, a village not far from the city of Neumarkt in der Oberpfalz. Visitors actually drove up with their tractors and the shed itself was divided into three clubs. There was the foxtrot area, the main dance floor and the hip-hop club. This one was relatively large at about 650 square feet and it had a stage next to the DJ booth, which was separated from the dance floor by two wide steps. All our friends were there and we generally had a lot of fun. We always left around midnight and then we arrived in front of the club at around 1 o'clock. That was just the right time, since many of the rural patrons were already lined up at 8 p.m. and the crowds hardly died down for the next four hours. When I was out with my boys, we sometimes even took the train to the village of Postbauer. That was fine. However, I was often in trouble when I went somewhere on my own with Deutsche Bahn. For example, when I was traveling by train from an event in Saarbrücken, two male officers from the Federal Police came into the train compartment. Although there were six people in total, they headed straight for me and asked for my ID. When I handed it to one of the officers, he went to the middle of the compartment and asked for my details so that everyone could hear. After everything was fine and I got my ID back, I got upset and accused them of racism. They just laughed and got off the train. In my compartment there was a woman who had observed the scene. She sat down opposite me and introduced herself as a Saxon MP. She also accused the officers of racism and offered to testify on my behalf if I wanted to press charges. I refused. It wouldn't do any good, I told her, and thanked her for the support she offered. As a teenager and an adult, I had to endure checks again and again. In the 90s it was especially bad. As soon as I drove into a city, no matter which one, there was a "general identity check". I am not an exception, I share this experience with countless other Black men. A policeman once talked to me openly and did not mince his words. He explained to me: "Black and southern-looking men commit more crimes per se than Germans. If officers happen to meet one, they take down the personal data, because he might have done something wrong, and then it's good to have the information at hand." I replied that statistically, the most common crimes are committed by *white* people. Maybe he should rather stand in front of a bank and ask for the personal data of all customers, because a bank robber could be among them. He didn't understand that. This is also a phenomenon of *white* racism: people do not understand or do not want to understand. Racism is group-based misanthropy. It affects Blacks, Asians, or other people who stand out in the majority *white* society primarily because of their appearance or cultural characteristics. This also applies to sexual orientation. The *white* majority is so full of prejudice that it does not accept the minorities. I now play out this clash between majority and minorities in my "Blue-Eyed" workshops. I learned the concept for this from Jane Elliott. Her workshop is based on an experiment that shows the harsh, unfair face of racism. Participants often burst into tears when they experience exclusion themselves for the first time and feel the pain that racism causes.

Back to the discotheque "Trend" and a Saturday that could not have started more beautifully and ended more horribly. It was a night that changed everything and set me far back in my emotional world. Carmen had spent the night before at my place. We rested all day. Around 11 p.m., we finally made our way to the village of Postbauer-Heng and were at the club shortly before midnight. But the atmosphere was unfortunately different from usual. Many of our friends were not there, so we didn't really have fun. We only danced a little bit and talked to a few acquaintances. Normally we stayed until the place closed, but now we were already on our way home around 3 o'clock.

Shortly before 4 o'clock in the morning we were back in the city of Lauf. I had just parked my gold Golf II in front of my parents' house, removed the key and turned to Carmen. Out of the blue, there was such a loud crash in the car that I spun around in shock. Something was hammering fiercly on my window pane. I was completely distraught and frightened. I looked into a dark, metallic something and didn't know what was going on. The voice I heard was soft and far away. The window was closed, after all, and in the dark I could only make out a shadowy figure. Suddenly someone yanked open my driver's door and a hand grabbed me by the wrist in a flash and tried to drag me out of the car. This didn't work, because first of all I was wearing a seatbelt and secondly I was well exercised, so I had built up a strong body tension. But somehow I had a kind of mental blackout. Anyway, I was standing out in the street without warning and was pressed against the Golf. My shoulders hurt and a male voice threatened me from behind with consequences if I didn't do as I was told. Carmen was talking to another guy standing with her. I didn't comprehend anything at all. I only noticed again how an uncontrollable rage rose in me out of helplessness. But I was ready to do anything to protect Carmen. When the guy behind me said that he was from the police and I was under arrest, I sagged for a moment, because at that instant I abruptly realized what was knocking on my window and what I was looking into. A damn muzzle. The cop was pointing a gun at me. I asked him why I was under arrest, and he told me we'd sort it out at the station. I looked at Carmen. She reassured me and indicated that I should just go along. So I went along, and since I must have seemed genuinely helpless, they put the handcuffs on me loosely. The journey to the police station took forever, although it was only about four minutes away by car from my parents' house. We drove through a gate, pulled into the secured parking lot, and went in to the back entrance of the station. The plainclothes policeman, who was talking to Carmen in front of the house, took me into a room where there was nothing except a table and a chair. No one answered my questions or explained what I was being charged with or what was going to happen to me. The officer just shook his head silently. I had lost all sense of time. At some point, a police officer in uniform entered the room and told me that it was 5:00 in the morning. And then he told me why I was here. The accusation: I was supposed to have robbed a cab in the city of Lauf at around 2 a.m.. I was stunned. "What did I do?!" I replied immediately. "We were still in the "Trend" at that time! And anyway, why would I do something like that?!"

I bombarded the officer with my questions and did not really notice that I was being escorted to the front desk of the police station. To the lineup. There I was in this bright room and when I saw who was standing in front of me, I got goose bumps. I was shaking and the feeling that had been holding me all these years was worse than ever: anger turned to sheer hatred! The robbed cab driver was a Turk I knew! When he saw me, he laughed at me with a nod of his head, turned to a police officer behind the counter and said, "I told you it was NOT Tibor, but a Black guy I didn't know!" Thereupon the unfriendly plainclothes cop, who had his back to me, turned around, grinned broadly and dirtily with his pancake face, and said, "Oh, your name is Tibor?" Since I was known known all over town and he gave my first and last name when he arrested me in front of my parents' house, I saw through this amateurish act and didn't respond at all. He came close to me – I was still handcuffed – and said that I should have better refrained from attacking a colleague. So there it was, the beginning of the revenge action of the fighter of that time. The friendly plainclothes policeman said something like "no offense" and asked me if I wanted a ride back. I didn't want that. I had to get rid of that feeling again. I thought I could clear my head again by walking home. Unfortunately, that didn't work. Carmen was very understanding and promised me to talk to her boss, the lawyer, about it. I pretended that this would put me at ease, but inside I was boiling. In those hours, a lot of things shattered for me. My trust in the rule of law, the police and in the city of Lauf an der Pegnitz as my hometown was lost. Once again I had been torn out of my, at least for a time, intact world. I was now facing an unknown opponent who was apparently much stronger than I was. Panic spread through me and dominated me from then on for many years. Since my involuntary visit to the police station, Germany was no longer a safe country for me, and that was and is also the case for other BPoCs.

Until today, until this book, I have not talked to anyone about all these experiences. While there were witnesses to some episodes around me, I don't think anyone grasped the full magnitude of it. We Black people pay a heavy price for being born with more melanin in our skin.

It's bad when many *white* people claim about us that we all look "the same." They never tire of claiming that it's "not so bad" or "no offense at all" to use terms like n*****, bimbo (i.e. darkie) or M*****kopf (German pejorative term for a small chocolate-covered cake filled with foamy sugar)." But anyone who argues like this is obstructing an even-handed discussion. We should all be clear about this: Everyday racism is an inherent part of Germany and every other country. Even as children, we acquire racist mental patterns. If someone decides to become a government official, for example, he or she does not simply discard the prejudiced thinking when they put on their uniform for the first time. Of course, police officers are no longer children; they think like adults and independently. But they move within fixed, established structures in which there are also certain attitudes and rules. Every day, they are confronted with the emotions and common opinions of their colleagues. This can have a contagious effect and influences their own thinking and actions. There may be some things that police officers experience more often in some communities and environments, but that doesn't mean that all Black people deal drugs or guns, for example. I was not born an angry Black man. I didn't learn to defend myself for fun. I never wanted to be so full of anger, hate and helplessness.

I met a lot of Black people during my travels in Germany. A Black Nazi who walked with them in Bavaria during the marches of extreme right-wing groups. Some Black people who told me they had never experienced racism. These I called "Steve" like Steve Urkel from the TV show "Family Matters". Because if you live in your world virtually blind to racism, then no one can change it. A lot of Black people I met are involved in Black communities. Unfortunately, there are also some Black people who, like me, are growing up alone in a *white* world and are disoriented about their skin color and family history. To you, I advise you to open up. I know how hard that is but the opportunities to share and network are much better today than they were for me in the 80s and 90s. It was 1999 and I was on my way to a club in Nuremberg. I was walking along a grassy sidewalk that led from the parking lot to the club building. After about 500 yards, a dark gray VW Golf shot across the grassy strip and stopped a few inches in front of me. Two guys jumped out and I automatically took a defensive position. "We know that one," a voice said. "Hands on the vehicle, spread your legs," yelled another. I was still on high alert. My hands were still on the hood and my legs were spread. The two men were undoubtedly plainclothes cops, one came very close to my ear and whispered, "Well, remember me? You were lucky then, only now it's my turn." I still had no idea who was talking to me and said so. "I'm the fellow from the field, back then, with Gustav." I had to grin. Why, I don't know to this day. He then became angry and articulate. "We'll definitely take you to the station and then I'll leave you in the cell until Sunday, bimbo (i.e. darkie)." Furiously, I tensed every muscle. What happened next was completely unforeseen. The two of them got a radio call, rushed to the Golf, got in and drove away with blue lights flashing. There I was, once again put through the wringer by racist policemen. I had had enough once and for all.

8. Off to a new world

The experience with the two plainclothes policemen reverberated like a trauma and had destroyed a lot in me. I distrusted people even more and I noticed that the city of Lauf an der Pegnitz sucked the air out of me. I became a traveler. I was looking for freedom, wanted to be the person I was somewhere, deep inside me. And I wished for a world in which I was treated more fairly. My anger was like an ocean, coming and going as in waves, ebbing and rising. My family fueled my emotions even more whenever I had to deal with them. One day, for example, I was supposed to pick up M. from my most Christian aunt, Tina, in Baden-Württemberg. I got into a traffic jam and was two hours delayed. M. was already waiting for me at the door, quite the angry person she could be. The trip back took two and a half hours and M. didn't speak a word to me. I knew that well enough and I was glad about it. When she arrived at her home, she called her sister Tina and said that the highway was not busy. My oh so Christian, devout aunt replied : "He's just an asshole." M. readily agreed with her. Is that the way you are born? Or made that way? And was I really an asshole because a traffic jam had cleared up after three hours? And was that the kind of thing you said to your nephew and about your son? Again and again I collided with them because I didn't do what they expected of me.

Theodor Wonja Michael (†) once told me that he had survived National Socialism as a Black young man only by assimilation. He obediently stopped at every red light, even in the middle of the night when no car had been on the road for hours. He also completely blanked out his Blackness. He ignored the African part of himself and was "*whiter* than the *whitest white* man." He was so law-abiding that it was grotesque. I thought hard about that after our brief conversation. I didn't know my Black part at all, how could I have discarded it? I even did the opposite and invented a Black father for some time. Out of self-protection I played a role in order not to be hurt anymore. But I was also clearly not a *white* man. Several people expected "exotic" stereotypes and "typical" Afro behavior from me. My height made me a basketball player, my deep voice made me a rapper, my sense of rhythm made me a dancer, and so for years I fulfilled every stereotype. I saw Black men on TV and replicated their behavior. Through friends and acquaintances from the USA I learned English and got used to the proper gestures. But I never saw myself as a unique person with a free spirit. I was a duplicate, a mix of Will Smith and Denzel Washington. At that time I would have been happy if Paps and M. had paid for an exchange year in America instead of sending me to the expensive private school. It was a lot better than the previous junior high school because of the multi-ethnicity, but it didn't give me any "empowerment" either. I had no idea what being Black meant, yet I was expected to act Black. But where was I supposed to be able to do that? It felt wrong, but I got used to taking on that role for myself. What else was I supposed to say or do in a relationship? Like, "Hey, I grew up in a *white* world – and came out of rape." What would that have triggered in my partner? Pity? Disgust? I certainly didn't want to show weakness. This dysfunctional relationship with myself and my skin color affected all areas of my life. I was constantly insecure and still had to act the strong man. I could not have an honest relationship for decades. For that, I sincerely apologize to the women I hurt. As soon as I got into situations where feelings were or should be expressed, I ran away or stonewalled. I didn't receive feminine, lasting loving closeness as a child, and when I did later, I couldn't handle it. This was a common theme throughout my life. I was a likable, good-looking unapproachable guy who didn't allow for real intimacy, yet at the same time cried out for it. The more police operations I had to experience, the more closed off I became. I couldn't talk about what was stirring me up inside.

I don't have a straight CV because racism is not linear. Because I was looking for my place in the world, I became a rapper, a Brothers Keeper, a prisoner. Because I needed to defend my life, I obtained a Master's in Face Reading, I was an actor, and finally I found myself as an anti-racism coach with the "Blue-Eyed" workshop series. I feel comfortable there. I show *white* participants the harsh and relentless face of racism. Experiencing it firsthand opens up new perspectives and creates space for the understanding I've wanted all my life. My journey is far from over. As a family man, I got a new job that couldn't be harder. Now I have little mice that I want to protect from everything bad. It's a tricky job. They gave me back the optimism that had disappeared for more than three decades. A phrase by Carlos Castaneda, a great writer, comes to mind: "To assume the responsibility of one's decisions means that one is ready to die for them." The question of what decision I would take if I knew I only had a short time to live gave me a clear view of what was important. Germany hasn't been my home country for a long time – and it never will be. I am tired of arousing associations in people. I don't want to see them work themselves up into fears anymore and worry that I might do something to them or steal something. These women who pull up their bags and hold on tightly are repugnant to me. Nowhere did I meet people who were skeptical or fearful of me more often than in Germany. The chapter Germany is closed – I am done with this country.

My relationship with the police remains ambivalent. As a Black German, I have had umpteen problematic inspections with about 50 to 70 officers. There was no reason for any of them. In addition, there was the undoubtedly racist harassment of the fighter from the field and his friends in uniform. All this made me alert. For many years I had pure fear: police vehicles meant the danger of losing my rights and freedom because of the color of my skin. On the other hand, I had been cooperating with the Bavarian police when I was a successful basketball player. With the youth police we planned the "My Way Fair Play" streetball tournament. Udo Nagel was my contact officer and the collaboration with him and the team was successful and friendly. Police officers also experience this ambivalence with people of dark skin. For example, they encounter a few Black violent offenders, but they also have Black colleagues with whom they work well. Nevertheless, the right-wing conservative group dynamics of some departments have an impact on individual officers. Those who are affected experience very clearly that racism in the police is a structural problem. I have learned: where there are free and openly chanting right-wing extremists, the executive often shows strange behavior as well. I had one of the worst controls in the city of Wurzen. As a Black person, you don't necessarily want to go there anyway. It is also peculiar in the outskirts of Leipzig, where swastika flags are displayed uncensored at flea markets and all visitors see that. As long as there are such and other dangerous places, my doubts about the seriousness of politicians in the fight against group-related misanthropy increase.

Some day-to-day racist clichés and statements I experience and hear again and again. Almost at the end, I describe my very personal view on this:

"You're not that Black after all!"

I don't know how people can think they're being nice when they tell me I'm not really brown/Black/whatever! Where the hell do you get the idea that someone can appreciate being told that he/she is something **not**?!

"Africa is responsible for its own poverty."

I firmly believe that the poverty and famines in Africa are a direct result of colonization and the slave trade. When you take the strongest men and the children out of a society, the women are left behind with the elderly population. There was no defense against hostile tribes and hunting was only done by the strongest men. People were traded for profit and the exploitation of the colonies is largely responsible for the composition of the local society. Now you can't pretend that they themselves sent the men away and let the children lie lazily in the huts. The rich north must bear the responsibility.

"Go back where you came from!"

Your thinking is so Neanderthal that you should be in a cave with a bludger. No German originated in this part of the country! So keep raging, citizen.

"This is sheer slave labor!" (When doing unwanted work.)

The Internet offers a huge trove of knowledge – including accounts of the lives of slaves. If you are really interested in what terrible criminal acts you associate with this phrase, read or watch videos on YouTube.

"You only got the job because you're a person of color!"

The term "colored" is racist. It is an attempt to define people as of a different color and as deviating from the *white* norm. Saying you only got the job because of the color of your skin devalues personal accomplishments and ignores how often

Black people are discriminated based on the color of their skin. Indeed, I did NOT get my desired job in the *white* majority because of the color of my skin. When privileged, *white* people portray themselves as victims by uttering such a statement, it is pathetic and severely dysfunctional in my eyes. I realize that many people who know me and thankfully read the book had no idea of my hidden side and secrets. This is not surprising. Either we had a good time together or my acting talent came into play. Since the age of seven, I lived with and through repression.

Involuntarily and in an expansive mood, I learned how I was supposed to have come into being. To this day I cannot come to terms with that. It was never clarified. I will probably die with the thought that a beast might be lurking in me. This condition is unforgivable, unbearable but also unchangeable.

M. will always remain a part of my life – but that is no longer relevant to me.

Thanks to the marching band of TSV Lauf. You gave me a trouble-free time. I would like to thank Olaf, Heiner, Nico, Marion, Ralph and Kerstin, Schorsch, Basine, Lichti and many other good, kind people. You don't care about skin colors and that was as valuable for me as the oasis for a desert people.

My friend Richie, aka the Greek. Thank you for your steadfast friendship. For over 30 years I have been able to rely on you at all times even though we now live in different states. You only meet friends like this once in a lifetime.

Thank you Harry and Gina Belafonte. You have given me

the true consciousness of a responsible Black man. Through you I became a great deal freer.

My friend H.L.W. Through you I learned about wanderlust and vegetarian food. Your light-hearted nature and cosmopolitan image you have maintained until today as well as a sincere friendship with me.

The last thanks of this book goes to my dad. Thank you for being so patient and loving with me. Thank you for sitting on the floor in front of me for hours when I was potty trained as a two year old. Thank you for telling me to try music and always encouraging me to love life. I failed you many times and hope that through this book you understand what was and still is going on with me. If it wasn't for you, I would no longer be in this world, that's for sure. Thank you for being the best dad a kid could have.

"Prejudice is the emotional commitment to ignorance."
(Nathan Rutstein)